HAUNTED RENO

HAUNTED RENO

JANICE OBERDING

Haunted
America

Published by Haunted America
A Division of The History Press
Charleston, SC 29403
www.historypress.net

Copyright © 2015 by Janice Oberding

Front cover: Courtesy Bill Oberding.

All rights reserved

First published 2015

Manufactured in the United States

ISBN 978.1.62619.948.4

Library of Congress control number: 2015943861

CONTENTS

CONTENTS

FOREWORD

Reno will always be a city I love, and it is my fervent hope that one day it will be the bustling city that is deeply etched in the museum of my mind.

Reno of the 1960s was a great place to be, with neon so bright one never knew the time of day. The two big clubs, Harold's and Harrah's, brought in some of the best entertainment, my favorites being Ray Anthony and his Bookends, Louis Prima, Judy Lynn and Jimmy Wakely. Also, there were the Mapes and the Riverside, where I had the pleasure of hearing a young Paul Anka belt out his tunes "Put Your Head on My Shoulder" and "Diana."

If those lonely streets, once awash with music of every genre and the laughter of people having a good time, could only talk. They might tell stories of the greats and near greats who once graced the Biggest Little City. Now, late at night, the only noises one might hear are the Washoe Zephyrs and the flowing Truckee River.

And there are the ghosts—Janice's book takes a look at the haunted and historic side of Reno. As you sit reading these pages, remember Marilyn Monroe and Clark Gable, as Reno was the location of their last movie. And think of all the broken hearts, those who, after divorces were granted, tossed rings that once held such promise into the river from the Wedding Ring Bridge.

Whether you are a Reno resident or a visitor, you can expect to spend some time on the haunted side of this city while visualizing glimpses of its past.

—Bonnie Harper

ACKNOWLEDGEMENTS

Writing is lonely work. The writer works alone, and yet no book would come to fruition without the help of others. There are many people I wish to acknowledge and thank for their help in this book (and other books as well). First, I must thank my lovely mother, Bonnie Harper, who took an old typewriter and a ream of paper and forged a writing path for me to follow. Mama's love of books and writing is part of my earliest and most cherished memories, and her encouragement and guidance have seen me through some challenging days and nights of writing. Thank you to my one-in-a-million husband, Bill, who is always there for me, who understands even when I'm antisocial, oblivious and writing; his suggestions and photography are invaluable. Thanks to my beautiful sister Diane Grulke, a writer herself, whose help with research, writing conversations and suggestions are deeply appreciated. Thank you to my dear friend Terri Hall-Peltier, whose friendship I treasure as much as I do her willingness to photograph, share her experiences and explore. Thanks are also due to my dear friend Deborah Carr-Senger for her encouragement, the road trips, writing suggestions and her wit and charm. Thanks also to my friends Mona Hoppe and Denise Barton Rodriguez for helping with some Reno research. Special thanks to my dear sweet friend Virginia Ridgway, whose ideas and wisdom have guided me in the right direction—most of the time. Thanks to my daughter-in-law Peggy, who accompanied me on many early ghost walks and ghost hunts, and to the many ghost investigators who have shared my enthusiasm for hunting ghosts over the years. Finally, since no book would get published without a publisher's go ahead, I want to thank Artie Crisp and the people at The History Press for saying yes to my ideas and for bringing them to viable book form.

INTRODUCTION

Reno's ghosts are a colorful lot. Like most of those in the western United States, they are of somewhat newer vintage than those of Gettysburg and New Orleans. But why compare ghosts and hauntings in the first place? Every city has its own legends, its history, its stories and its haunted places.

Reno is the "Biggest Little City in the World." Like Paris and Chicago, a river runs through it, but that is where the similarities end. Reno is different, unlike any other city in the country, and yet the city is, in many ways, as mundane as a Monday morning coffee klatch. This doesn't override Reno's endearing one-of-a-kind feel. It is not nearly as large as Las Vegas in the southern part of the state. Nonetheless, Reno has something special.

Recently Reno was unfairly proclaimed the most depressed city in the world. This is a city in flux. Its downtown area has enjoyed a resurgence of popularity in the last decade. More cosmopolitan than before, the train trench and numerous condo conversions have made downtown living a reality. It's a reality buyers have opted for. While the face of the city has changed, some of its historic downtown buildings have avoided demolition. Yes, there is work to be done, certainly. But with a newly elected young and vibrant mayor at the helm, we will get there.

Reno is my town. I grew up here, got married here and raised my two sons here. In other words, I am staying. During the summer and early fall, my husband, Bill, and I do the Reno Ghost Walk in downtown Reno. And ghosts are where this book comes in. Of the many things Reno is known for, its haunted locations are not among them. For this is Nevada, and in

Nevada (particularly in Las Vegas), old buildings that may be a haven for ghosts and hauntings are quickly demolished in favor of newer, bigger and brighter edifices. And what do the displaced ghosts do? Why, they probably opt to reside at the same locations. You see, just because a building is brand sparkling new doesn't mean it's not haunted.

Someone once wisely observed that ghosts are everywhere. And they are. Wherever people have lived and died, dreamed and dined and danced and done all the things that make life interesting, that's where we'll find ghosts. Indeed, they are everywhere, not necessarily confined to the creepy old moss-covered cemeteries you'll find in old black-and-white movies of yore, although some ghosts may choose to haunt such places, just as some living people choose to live in the suburbs rather than the city.

The ghosts of Reno reside in several varied locations. Some, like that of Marilyn Monroe, apparently relocate when the mood strikes. Look at this as the ghostly version of a snowbird who packs up when the winter comes and chases warmer climes.

Ghosts and history go hand in hand. Before we move on to the hauntings, I should tell you how the name Biggest Little City in the World came to be. "You'll like Reno" and "Where the Old West Still Lives" were two early slogans used by the city of Reno to promote tourism. With the completion of the nation's first transcontinental highway, the Lincoln Highway, in 1927, Reno looked for something to suitably impress its travelers. An arch was the answer.

On the night of June 25, 1927, Governor Balzar threw the switch that lit up Reno's first arch. Later, Reno mayor E.E. Roberts suggested a contest for a new Reno slogan that could be added to the arch.

"Reno, the Thriving" and "Town Without a Frown" were two of the suggested slogans. Even after the mayor's office was flooded with over five hundred entries, city officials could not decide on a slogan that would best tout Reno's superiority. After nearly a year of indecisiveness, the chamber of commerce offered a $100 prize for the best slogan; if that didn't bring in a good slogan, it was reasoned, nothing would.

G.A. Burns of Sacramento, California, was the winner with "The Biggest Little City in the World." Mayor E.E. Roberts pointed out that this was not the first time such a slogan had been used. In 1910, promoters of the Johnson/Jefferies fight proclaimed Reno to be "The Biggest Little City on the Map." Roberts hoped for something more original.

"It has slam!" E.H. Walker, manager of the Reno Chamber of Commerce, said regarding "The Biggest Little City in the World" slogan. Slam or not, Reno's now famous slogan was added to the arch in 1929. The city is named for General Jesse Lee Reno, a Union officer who was killed in battle during the Civil War. Reno wasn't the city's first name; it was originally called Lakes Crossing for businessman Myron Lake. After General Reno's heroic death, several cities honored the fallen soldier by naming, or renaming, themselves after him. Never mind that General Jesse Lee Reno never set foot in this town bisected by the Truckee River. Abraham Lincoln never visited or dreamed of all the places and things that would one day honor him, either.

In his 1766 *Dreams of a Spirit Seer*, German philosopher Immanuel Kant wrote, "Ghost stories are always listened to and well received in private, but pitilessly disavowed in public."

People are curious about ghosts. This is nothing new. This curiosity may be inherent, I don't know. But what I do know is that some so-called coincidences are too overwhelming to accept as that and nothing more. Stories of ghosts and spirits are found in nearly every culture. Many of the different languages spoken throughout the world today have at least one word that translates to mean ghost or spirit.

Many of the world's greatest philosophers wondered if the dead could return to this earthly plane and whether we, the living, can communicate with them. Aristotle and Socrates spoke at length on their regular conversations with those in the spirit world.

In a letter to a friend, Italian poet Dante Alighieri (1265–1321) wrote that his masterpiece *The Divine Comedy* was "the state of souls after death." It's been said that the final cantos might never have come to light if his apparition hadn't appeared before his son and told him where it was hidden.

Eighteenth-century Swedish philosopher and theologian Emanuel Swedenborg (1688–1772) wrote several volumes on his "spiritual" visions and what they meant. One of his well-documented visions involved a fire some sixty miles from his location. Sixty miles was quite a distance in 1759. Yet Swedenborg was able to describe in vivid detail a raging fire as it burned. More importantly, he said that a particular friend's home had been reduced to ashes and went on to stun those around him by declaring the precise hour that the fire would be contained.

A few days later, a messenger from the faraway town would confirm the accuracy of Swedenborg's vision, even down to the time of the fire being put out.

Today's ghost-hunting buzzword is evidence. With all our scientific equipment, we should be able to produce evidence, right? In his book *Contact with the Other World*, James H. Hyslop wrote, "The absence of evidence for survival is not evidence of the absence of it."

I agree with that. However, in writing this book, I wanted first and foremost to inform and entertain. The proving of ghostly existence I'll leave to the more technical among us.

In Shakespeare's *Romeo and Juliet*, Juliet says the line, "What's in a name? That which we call a rose by any other name would smell as sweet."

And so it is with ghosts. Whether they are spirit, entity, disembodied spirit, graveyard apparition, a wisp of cold air, the vision of a dead loved one or a voice that emanates from nowhere—all of these, and more, can be ghosts. For the purpose of this book, I have generally used the word "ghost" to describe any anomalous occurrence. Ghosts are truly everywhere, and Reno has its fair share.

So snuggle into a comfy reading spot and let's take a look at Reno's ghosts. You're about to discover that not only is Reno the Biggest Little City in the World, but it's also a haunted city.

Chapter 1

CRIME AND PUNISHMENT

THE 601 AND A DOWNTOWN LYNCHING

When you think of lynching, you generally think of the Wild West, back in the days when gunslingers and cattle rustlers ruled the streets. Either that, or long-ago racist elements in other parts of the country where a man might be lynched based solely on the color of his skin. I'd be willing to bet that few people think of downtown Reno as the location of a lynching. But it happened.

The old iron bridge that crossed the Truckee River in downtown Reno is long gone. Its 1905 replacement is set for demolition sometime in the near future. In all likelihood, the ultra-modern bridge that will replace it will also be haunted by the shadowy figure of an angry and confused man. He is the ghostly Luis Ortiz, and he seeks the justice that he didn't receive in life.

The lynching of Luis Ortiz took place on Reno's downtown iron bridge one September night in 1891. The secret vigilante group, known as the 601, had no patience for lawyers and trials (although some of them might well have been lawyers or judges). Like the 601 of Virginia City and that of Carson City, Reno's group was composed of several prominent male citizens who wanted swift justice done. If that meant taking matters into their own hands, so be it. They aimed to keep their community safe and free of violence one way or another. If a man threatened Reno's tranquility, the 601 Vigilance Committee would be ready.

Luis Ortiz was a young Winnemucca ranch hand who turned mean after a few whiskeys. He severely injured three men in a knife fight and was convicted of assault in July 1891. He was a problem that Reno didn't need. So Constable Dick Nash escorted Ortiz to a westbound train and saw him off. Luis Ortiz would be another town's problem, or so Constable Nash thought. But he was wrong.

Luis liked Reno. He came back to town on September 17, 1891. But first things first, Luis stopped in at the nearest saloon, at the Grand Central Hotel on the corner of Plaza and Virginia Streets in downtown Reno. One whiskey after another fueled his mean temper. As the hours wore on, he grew angrier and started looking for a fight. But no one obliged him—no man was that stupid. Around midnight, Luis was told that the saloon was closing, but he didn't want to go elsewhere to drink, so he pulled his gun and fired wildly. Constable Nash arrived, accompanied by two men, and tried to subdue Ortiz. Nothing doing—Ortiz was not to be subdued, nor was he going to jail. All he wanted was a drink and a fight. Looking Nash in the eye, he raised his pistol and fired, striking him in the stomach.

Constable Nash was taken to a doctor's house, and Luis was taken to jail. A day passed. While the well-respected constable clung to life, bad news broke. There was no hope for Nash; his doctor said his patient's injuries would prove fatal. When questioned in jail by reporters, Luis Ortiz claimed it had all been a blur. He had been so drunk he couldn't remember a thing. This, of course, did not help Constable Nash. The 601 was listening. Justice must prevail. They sprang into action. And Luis Ortiz would pay.

They waited until the town was sleeping and then went to the jailhouse for Ortiz. Deputy John Caughlin was tricked into opening the jail door. Once he did so, he was overcome by the mob.

"Ortiz, you are wanted downtown," one of the men said.

Those words meant but one thing. With their frightened prisoner struggling to get away, they crept to the Virginia Street Bridge.

"Do you have any final requests, Ortiz?" someone asked.

"A priest and a glass of water."

A man proffered a whiskey flask. "Whiskey's all we have."

Ortiz gulped. Trembling, he told them where to send his personal effects and bravely faced his executioners.

"Ready," he announced firmly.

The next morning, Ortiz's lifeless body was cut down from the bridge. Miraculously, Constable Nash made a full recovery. The *Weekly Gazette Stockman* of September 1891 had this to say about the affair: "Ortiz Hung! The County and Town well rid of a worthless vagabond. The man who was so handy with his gun departs this life at the end of a rope."

Present-day view of the Ortiz lynching location and downtown Reno. *Photo by Bill Oberding.*

As for those who took part in the murder of Luis Ortiz, no one was ever arrested or even questioned about that night. And as you might suspect, no one ever publicly admitted to having been anywhere near the iron bridge on the night of September 24, 1891. Obviously, the ghostly Luis Ortiz wants justice. He aimlessly wanders the bridge seeking answers. He has the habit of rushing up to someone as if to ask a question and then turns and wanders away. Those who don't see Luis Ortiz have sensed his unhappy presence on the northwest side of the bridge.

Sometime before October 15, 1905, when the new bridge was erected, a tourist who'd heard of the Ortiz lynching went to the bridge and asked for a sign from Ortiz's ghost. He got one. A spider dropped down and bit the man on the neck. Was it Luis or was it a coincidence?

Now, if you think it's a coincidence, let me tell you this. One night during the ghost walk, we had a group of about twenty on the bridge, and we were telling the Luis Ortiz story. When we got to the part about the spider, a woman gasped and jumped. She'd been bitten on the ankle—by a spider, presumably.

At this writing, the old 1905 Wedding Ring Bridge is being demolished and a new bridge is being erected. As he did with the 1905 bridge, Luis Ortiz will probably continue his lonely trek on this new bridge, still seeking justice.

THE GHOST OF JOSEPH ROVER

There's a reason that J.W. Rover's ghost is usually spotted around the Washoe County Courthouse. He was hanged in the courtyard on a snowy February morning in 1878. Today, that area is the new courthouse annex, so any comments about a ghostly man skulking in that area of the building are assumed to be sightings of Joseph Rover.

Nowadays, state executions are carried out at the state prison in Carson City, but in the late nineteenth century, those judged guilty were generally executed in the county of their crime. So it was with Rover. He had been convicted of murdering his business partner, L.N. Sharp, out in the Black Rock Desert. But the case was appealed to the Nevada Supreme Court, which overturned it on a technicality and ordered a retrial. The second trial ended with Rover being found guilty of first-degree murder. A second appeal was made to the Nevada Supreme Court, which once again found for the appellant. The judge had given wrong instructions in defining reasonable doubt. The third time was not a charm for Joseph Rover. His third trial resulted in a hung jury. A fourth trial was held, and Rover was found guilty of murder in the first degree and sentenced to die.

All hope was gone for Rover—unless his attorneys could convince a special sheriff's jury that he was insane. If they did so, Rover would rot in prison—dismal, but a better alternative to hanging.

You sometimes have to wonder at people of earlier times. How a public execution could draw a crowd of otherwise civilized people is a question for a sociologist to answer. Suffice it to say, there were many onlookers gathered in the Washoe County Courthouse to await the jury's finding. The sheriff's jury pondered the facts, and after four hours, a decision was reached. Rover was as sane as any man. And he would die for the grisly dismemberment murder of L.N. Sharp.

With the verdict, Sheriff Kinkead saw no reason to delay any further. Rover naturally disagreed. When Sheriffs Kinkead and Lamb came to escort him to the gallows, he began to weep. Trembling, he stood and nearly collapsed. Father Pettit and Father Twormey assisted him as he shuffled toward doom. The two priests would stay on the scaffold and pray with him until the very end. This was some small comfort, and he slowly walked up the gallows' steps and seated himself in the only available chair.

The first and only execution in Reno would take place in the courtyard, hidden from public view by a tall fence. Sheriff Kinkead had invited two hundred men to witness the execution, and they shivered in the cold.

Asked if he had anything to say, Rover said, "Gentlemen—I have nothing much to say; I am so prostrated by this long persecution, that I am unable to say what I desire to, and the time too, will not admit of it…"

He spoke there in the bitter cold for fifty-two more minutes, claiming it was a conspiracy between the state's attorney and his accuser. McWorthy was the actual killer. Sheriff Lamb placed the rope around his neck, and Sheriff Kinkead placed the black hood over his head.

"Oh! Lamb…" Rover said softly.

He didn't get the chance to finish his sentence. The signal was given and the trap sprung. The *Daily Nevada State Journal* of February 20, 1878, said of his execution, "He has gone, and with his death the law is satisfied. Let us all think as charitably as possible of the deceased, who has gone where none but his God can judge him."

But J.W. Rover's ghost was not satisfied. He was on a mission. Now the ghostly man would proclaim his innocence from the spirit realm. Within a week of the hanging, the *Reno Gazette* printed the following story.

ROVER VISITS MRS. BOWERS
Mrs. Bowers, the Washoe seeress called on Gen. Clark the other day and said to him, "General, Rover was innocent."
"How do you know?" said he.

She answered. "I was eating dinner when someone tapped me on the shoulder and I heard a voice say, 'I am J.W. Rover, and have just been hanged in Reno, but I am innocent.'" Until this visit Mrs. Bowers declares that she did not know that Rover had been hanged. Since this occurrence the Carson spiritualists have held three or four séances; Rover is called for, appears and tells the same old story, so oft repeated.

Eilley Bowers had a reputation as an eccentric old woman. Her assertions were not considered accurate. After all, how often is much attention paid to the word of ghosts and those who converse with them? Twenty years passed. Some still questioned the guilt or innocence of Rover. The following story appeared in the July 24, 1899 issue of the *Reno Gazette*:

SLIGHTLY MISTAKEN
The Carson News *says that McWorthy, the rabbit hole Sulphur man, who early in the '70s was the principle prosecuting witness in the trial of J.W. Rover for the murder of I.N. Sharp at Rabbit Hole, Humboldt Count, died in Arizona a few years ago and confessed to being the murderer of Sharp, who Rover was hung for killing, in the Court House yard of Washoe County. The* News *is mistaken, for McWorthy is alive today and living in Oakland. Rover killed Sharp and paid the penalty with his own life.*

Was J.W. Rover guilty? We will never know. If he were innocent, this could be a case of unfinished business as far as his ghost is concerned. A shadowy apparition has been seen in the annex area of the courthouse and out near the side of the building—still trying to proclaim his innocence, no doubt. The same thing can be said if he were guilty. The old adage "There are no guilty people in prison" might apply here. Either way, J.W. Rover's ghost walks the area.

BABY FACE NELSON, AKA LESTER GILLIS

There is a commonly accepted theory regarding ghosts: if you were a good person in life, you will be a good person in death. The opposite holds true. Bad person equals bad ghost. Imagine, then, how hateful the ghost of Baby Face Nelson can be. But wait a minute—Baby Face Nelson was a Chicago

Prohibition gangster turned killer who met his demise in Barrington, Illinois. Why would his ghost be haunting an alley in Reno?

Baby Face Nelson lived in Reno briefly. During that time, he went by the name Jimmy Burrell, and he worked as a chauffeur and nightclub bouncer for two of Reno's most notorious underworld figures, James McKay and William Graham, who incidentally worked for George Wingfield. Prohibition was the law of the land, and gaming had not yet been legalized in Nevada. This didn't matter to Graham and McKay, who ran illegal gambling operations, saloons and brothels. In Reno, if it was illegal, these two men were involved. Baby Face was a natural who is believed to have played a role in Reno's most famous disappearance, that of Roy Frisch. But we'll get to that story later. Let's get to that alley, which runs alongside Sundance Books all the way to the Nevada Museum of Art, a block or so away.

Graham lived in a mansion on California Avenue, cattycorner to the alley where the ghostly gangster has been seen running from south to north. The apparition never acknowledges anyone and always seems to be in a big hurry. In life, Nelson probably took this route to and from his employer's home many times. He may have been late for work at the nightclub or trying to escape what he saw as danger. This repetition could have led to what is referred to as place memory. It is a ghost of sorts, not interactive but more like a movie in which one scene replays itself over and over. Don't be alarmed if you should encounter the ghostly gangster, and certainly don't waste your time trying to communicate with him, either.

MA BARKER AND THE GANG

Was she just a sweet little old lady or the coldblooded matriarch of a ruthless gang of killers? That depends on whom you ask. For a time during the fall of 1933 and the spring of 1934, Ma Barker and two of her sons, as well as other members of the Karpis-Barker gang, chose to hang out in Reno.

Because they were in town at the time of Roy Frisch's disappearance, there was some speculation that members of the Karpis-Barker gang had taken part in it. Nothing was ever proven. Ma Barker and her sons lived quietly under the name of Blackburn in a small house on Pueblo Street. During the time they lived in Reno, the gang was rumored to have driven to California to rob banks. Yet another story that's gone around Reno for years concerns Ma Barker's violin case.

The notorious Ma Barker, or so the story goes, carried a gun around Reno hidden in a violin case. This may have been standard operating procedure for gangsters of that era, but it's doubtful that the matronly Ma actually toted a Tommy gun in such fashion. In fact, the woman the FBI dubbed "Bloody Mama," may not have been the ruthless gang leader at all. While J. Edgar Hoover referred to Ma as "a veritable beast of prey," her underworld friends remembered her as just an old woman who didn't have the smarts to plan such activities as kidnapping and bank robbing.

The FBI believed that Ma Barker and the gang had several friends in the Biggest Little City. In March 1934, FBI agents in Reno attempted to ensnare Ma and other members of the gang, but their efforts were thwarted by friends who tipped the gang off. It was this Reno connection that may have led to the final bloody confrontation with FBI agents. Ma and her son Fred were located by the FBI through letters that were mailed to Reno and then forwarded on to them in Florida by a friend.

On January 16, 1935, the FBI closed in on Ma and Fred's hideout cottage at Oklawaha, Florida. After a gun battle that lasted several hours, Ma and Fred were corpses. Upon hearing of her death, J. Edgar Hoover, who had a few skeletons rattling in his own closet, proclaimed Ma to be "a jealous old battle axe."

Ma Barker's friends in Reno wisely lay low, kept their mouths shut and never publicly claimed any connection to her. But like Baby Face Nelson, Ma Barker has chosen to return to the Biggest Little City. The specter of an elderly woman walking along Pueblo Street has been spotted numerous times since Ma met up with the Grim Reaper. No, she doesn't carry a violin case, and yes, there is a tendency to assume ghosts are those of well-known people. Still, I'd be willing to bet it's the ghostly Ma Barker looking for a likely bank.

PRISCILLA FORD'S THANKSGIVING DAY MASSACRE

I'm often asked about the most haunted location in Reno. I'm not sure of that, but a busy downtown sidewalk would have to be close. Too many people have heard heart-wrenching screams and felt overwhelming sadness, fear and nausea while walking on this sidewalk for it not to be so. Ghosthunters who use the K-2 meter can tell you that meter readings are usually erratic and high here. The deaths that occurred here were violent and unexpected. One minute you're in this plane, and the next...

Thanksgiving 1980 is one that Reno will never forget. The weather was mild. A throng of tourists crowded into downtown Reno for a three-day weekend of gaming fun. Legalized gambling was still in Nevada only; if one wanted to tempt Lady Luck, the choices were clear: Reno or Las Vegas. Along North Virginia Street, hotel/casinos were busy serving up traditional turkey dinners with all the trimmings. The aroma of roasted turkey wafted through the air. The sidewalks were bustling with people headed toward one casino or another, where gambling and food awaited. Those who had eaten their Thanksgiving feast were sitting at favorite blackjack tables, slot machines and Keno lounges; those who hadn't hungrily made their way toward casino coffee shops.

During their breaks, casino employees seeking a respite from stale cigarette smoke stepped out for a breath of fresh air. Some ducked in and out of other establishments, wishing friends a happy holiday, perhaps pulling the handles of promising slot machines or downing a quick fortifying drink. There were no computers keeping track. Liquor flowed freely among casino employees; a fistful of drink tokes for a fistful of drink tokes. What were friends for?

She had been in town only a few weeks, and she was furious. What would she do? A half bottle of wine later, she decided. The voices inside her head were telling her to kill. And she could not disobey. Fifty-one-year-old Priscilla Ford slowly drove her blue 1974 Lincoln Continental north on Virginia Street toward downtown.

The Lincoln inched past the Mapes and crossed First Street, then Second Street and then onto the sidewalk. The voices were louder now. She plowed through the crowd. Oblivious to the agonized screams of her victims and those of horrified onlookers, she drove on. Even as the Lincoln Continental tossed broken and battered bodies into the air, Priscilla Ford continued driving.

When she was just short of the arch, two men pulled their cars in front of the Lincoln to block her way. Only then, when forced to do so, did she stop.

Later, Ford was heard to say, "The more dead the better. I hope I got seventy-five. A Lincoln Continental can do a lot of damage, can't it?"

The carnage was horrific. Twenty-three people lay injured and maimed on the bloodied sidewalk in downtown Reno. Seven others were dead from the injuries they had sustained. After spending twenty-five years on Nevada's death row, Priscilla Ford died on January 29, 2005. She was seventy-five years old. Her state-level appeals had all been exhausted by 1989. However, she still had federal appeals available to her at the time of her death.

People who aren't aware of this area's history have told me that they've always crossed the street when coming to this section of the sidewalk. At least now they know why it makes them so uncomfortable.

COURTHOUSE SHOOTING

In his *Waste Land*, T.S. Eliot says, "April is the cruelest month, breeding lilacs out of the dead land—"

That might be so. But in Reno, November seems to be a cruel month. It is a month that's given rise to ghosts and hauntings, a month in which two horrendous crimes were committed very near or on Thanksgiving.

It was Wednesday, November 23, the day before Thanksgiving in 1960. Students eagerly awaited those two extra days away from school, harried housewives made last-minute preparations for the big day's feast and casino employees geared up for Reno's traditionally busy weekend. Two family men went to their jobs that day expecting to go home that night, expecting to celebrate Thanksgiving with family and friends. But something went terribly wrong.

At the Washoe County Courthouse, it was business as usual. The court calendar was filled; in an improvised courtroom on the second floor, attorneys Edwin Mulcahy, Eli Livierato and Sam Francovich were representing clients in an acrimonious land dispute case. Francovich represented Robert "the Sandman" Williams, Livierato his estranged wife and Mulcahy was counsel for Williams's despised mother-in-law. The case was being heard before Judge Jon Collins, who would later go on to become a Nevada Supreme Court chief justice.

This was in a more naïve time, a time before metal detectors scanned purses and personal belongings of anyone entering the courthouse. Judge Collins was, in his words, "apprehensive" of Robert Williams's behavior, so he asked bailiffs to search Williams before he entered the court. Unbeknownst to those who frisked him, Williams had secreted in a gun in a waistband holster.

Judge Collins also requested that a bailiff be present during the proceedings. With a bailiff out sick that day, the others handled the workload by covering more than one trial at a time. This they did by bouncing back and forth between courtrooms. When the bailiff stepped out to see about another courtroom, Williams's eyes glinted with rage. He was a well-known businessman, running a good sand and gravel business; there was no way he could lose out to his mother-in-law. Minutes ticked by on the wall clock at the back of the room. The room was silent as Judge Collins scanned his notes. Williams stared coldly at his wife and her mother. He could not lose. The judge cleared his throat and announced that Robert Williams and his wife were entitled to only a shared one-half ownership of the parcel of land, and Williams's mother-in-law was entitled to the other half.

Williams swore under his breath and noisily shifted his weight. Francovich urged him to be silent and to listen to the judge. But Williams was beyond listening to anything his attorney had to say. He leapt to his feet, pulled his gun and started firing wildly at his wife, who ducked beneath a table, and at his hated mother-in-law, Livierato and Mulcahy.

Francovich grabbed his client's arm and held it while a spectator wrested the gun from him. Judge Collins raced to a phone and summoned help. Eli Livierato fell backward mortally wounded. Mulcahy stumbled to the rear of the courtroom and fell over a railing that separated spectators from the attorney's area; he had been hit three times. Tom Krel,* a witness for Williams's mother-in-law, was hit in the shoulder and the buttock. Both Krel and Mulcahy remained conscious and alert while waiting for ambulances to arrive.

Police and deputies rushed in and quickly subdued Williams. As he was being led out, he asked, "What happened?"

The scream of police and ambulance sirens sent Virginia Street motorists scrambling to get out of the way.

Attendants raced into the courthouse and quickly assessed the situation in the makeshift courtroom. Krel and Mulcahy were able to talk about their wounds, but Livierato was not. A resuscitator was placed over the young attorney's mouth, but his life was quickly ebbing. A priest hurried into the courtroom and administered the last rites. The mood at the courthouse was somber. Employees and spectators cried softly in the hallways. This day that had started out like any other would end in unthinkable tragedy for two families.

At Washoe Medical Center, Mulcahy underwent surgery for several hours; he would linger for five more days. Like Eli Livierato, his friend and former classmate at Hasting Law School, Edwin Mulcahy left behind a wife and children. Reno was a much smaller town in 1960. Edwin Mulcahy was the executive secretary for the Nevada State Bar Association and a former assistant Washoe County district attorney. Both Livierato and Mulcahy were well liked and respected by their colleagues. Understandably, no attorney was anxious to represent the man responsible for their deaths.

---

* Not his real name.

Williams was held at the Washoe County Jail. For the first several hours after the shooting, he refused to speak or eat. Eventually, he broke his hunger strike and asked for an attorney. Las Vegan Harry Claiborne would handle Williams's defense.

Robert Williams stood trial in December 1961. Judge Collins appeared as a witness for the prosecution; he testified that Williams was "mean and mad…but he knew exactly what he was doing." Judge Collins also told the court that he had seen "tongues of flame from the muzzle. I heard all the shots in four or five seconds."

Williams was found guilty of murder in the first degree and sentenced to life without the possibility of parole. On the morning of February 18, 1973, he was rushed from prison to the Tahoe Carson Hospital after complaining of severe chest pains. He died in the hospital a week later.

Eli Livierato and Edwin Mulcahy are not forgotten at the Washoe County Courthouse. Visitors to the courthouse have probably seen the wall plaque that honors the two men whose lives were cut short so senselessly on that long-ago Wednesday afternoon.

This tragedy could well be the reason for the feelings of pain, fear and terrible sadness that some have felt in this area of the court.

DAYLIGHT BANK ROBBERY AND DARING ESCAPE FROM JAIL

On Friday, September 27, 1974, the Shriners were in town; at 6:30 p.m., their noisy parade began marching its way down North Virginia Street. As a large cheering crowd gathered on the downtown sidewalks, a green van pulled up in the alley behind the Nevada State Bank on the corner of Second Street and North Virginia Street. No one paid any attention to the three men who jumped out and ran for the door. Bank employees were busily wrapping up their tasks for the day when the three men entered the building through a basement door.

Assistant bank operations officer Megan Dren[†] and bank operations officer John Torg started downstairs to lock up the safety deposit vault. As Dren reached the last step, a man grabbed her roughly and pushed a gun into her ribs. The startled woman screamed.

"Shut up," he ordered, "or I'm going to kill you!"

[†] All employees names in this story have been changed.

Her assailant wasn't alone. Two men stood behind him; all three wore cheap Halloween masks, blue jumpsuits and rubber-soled shoes. While he held the gun pressed against her, one of his cohorts grabbed Torg.

"You," he told Dren, "are going to walk up the stairs and walk over to the man on the phone and tell him what's happening and to hang up."

She nodded her understanding, and they all walked upstairs to bank manager Fred Marl's desk. Marl looked up from the phone, and Dren nodded to the robbers. "I'll call you back," he spoke into the receiver. The person on the other end of the phone kept talking; Marl listened silently.

"If you don't get off that goddamn phone I'm going to shoot her," one of the robbers snapped angrily. Marl hung up the phone. The robbers ordered one of the tellers to open the cash drawers and then led all the employees to the vault and handcuffed them. When their duffle bags were stuffed full, the three robbers raced out to their getaway van. An hour later, the stolen vehicle was discovered in the parking garage at Sierra and Court Streets, across the street from the Washoe County sheriff's office.

The take was over $1 million, and according to the FBI, this was the largest bank robbery in United States history at that time. Bank robbing is a federal offense, and FBI agents converged on the downtown bank. While they interviewed the bank's employees and sifted through clues, police officers had their hands full with onlookers curious about what was going on in the bank.

In November, Sam Fells, John Sorgre and Floyd Clayton Forsberg were arrested by the FBI at a private residence in Newport Beach, California. Trial was set before federal judge Bruce Thompson at the federal court on Booth Street for June 2. But Floyd Clayton Forsberg had other ideas; he and another inmate escaped from the jail by climbing out a vent and placing a ladder across the roof of the jail to the Riverside Hotel.

Security was tight on the morning of the trial; a U.S. marshal from Sacramento set up a weapon detector outside the courtroom. Anyone coming into the hallway or that area of the courtroom would be electronically scanned for metal; this procedure, though standard practice today, was set up as a precaution only for the duration of this trial.

With Forsberg still missing, Fells and Sorgre appeared before Judge Thompson. Fells promptly pleaded guilty to the heist. He would be sentenced to twenty years for his part in the crime.

Sorgre claimed his constitutional rights had been violated when FBI agents arrested him in Newport Beach. He wanted certain evidence suppressed.

Judge Thompson ruled against him, and the evidence would be presented. After a short trial, Sorgre would walk away a free man after the jury voted to acquit him.

This left only Floyd Clayton Forsberg still at large. On the morning of June 29, 1975, Forsberg and his wife were holed up at the Riverside Motel in Bend, Oregon. In the adjoining room was Pete Weems, the accomplice who had aided Forsberg's escape from the Reno jail. The three fugitives were sleeping soundly at 3:30 a.m., when the doors suddenly crashed open and FBI agents surrounded them.

Everyone was accounted for, except for twenty-year-old Denise Catlin, who was known to be traveling with Forsberg. The trio steadfastly denied any knowledge of the young woman's whereabouts. And then the bank heist case took a strange turn.

In October, a woman's body was discovered in a shallow grave near Bend, Oregon. Authorities believed she was the missing traveling companion of Forsberg. When her identity was positively established, they charged Forsberg with her murder; he pleaded innocent, and a trial was set for July. In the meantime, he was convicted of the Reno bank robbery in federal court.

Forsberg's erstwhile pal Sam Fells took the stand and told the court how the three men had methodically planned the robbery. He was living in Sparks and drove by the bank every day when he took his girlfriend to work downtown. One day, he decided the bank would be an easy target.

"I just thought it could be robbed." He said. Then he went on to explain how he stopped in the bank to watch the habits of employees. "After a period of time, I told John Sorgre about it."

In April 1974, he shared his plan to rob the bank with Floyd Clayton Forsberg and his wife, who were staying in Las Vegas. But how had the robbers entered the bank so easily? With a key, of course. Fells told the court that he and Sorgre had gone to the bank months before the robbery to make a key. While Sorgre acted as lookout, he removed the lock from the bank door they would enter and replaced it with another lock.

"It took about three to five minutes—no longer than five minutes," he said. He took the bank's lock to a motel room, made a key for it and then took the lock back to the bank and replaced it. "The bank's lock was old, [and] some of the tumblers fell out and I had to replace them."

A few days before the robbery, he went back to the bank to make sure the lock hadn't been replaced. He and Forsberg then went to Sacramento, where they stole a green State of California van to use as their getaway vehicle. Back in Reno, they rented a small warehouse on Telegraph Street and stored the van and other robbery materials there until they robbed the bank.

Next up was Pete Weems, who testified how he helped Forsberg escape from Washoe County Jail; for his services, Wels was to be paid $20,000. After the escape, Forsberg, according to Wels, told him details about the robbery.

Forsberg was convicted of bank robbery. Before his scheduled murder trial date in Oregon, he changed his plea to guilty and was sentenced to life imprisonment at the Oregon State Prison. He was discharged in February 1994.

COURTHOUSE AND JAIL GHOSTS

Shortly after the bank robbery mentioned in the previous story, it was decided that the courthouse jail was antiquated and use of it should be discontinued. This didn't put a stop to the ghostly activity.

We were doing a daylight ghost walk for a friend and his family one summer Sunday afternoon when he decided he wanted to tour the courthouse and the jail upstairs. That wasn't going to happen, and we told him so. But he was undeterred, and he asked us to accompany him back to the side (Court Street) entrance of the courthouse. Once inside the door, he flipped out his Vegas Metro badge and the tour was on.

Did those showing us around believe in ghosts? No, they didn't. But our friend did, and as he asked them about the jail, they admitted that there were some strange things that took place up here at nighttime. For one thing, the heavy iron doors will open and bang shut of their own volition. And the footsteps—at all hours of the night, the footsteps of someone who seems to be pacing back and forth can clearly be heard.

"Ghosts?" we asked.

"No. I don't know what it is," one of the guards said.

Sobbing and moaning round out the phenomena that occur in the old courthouse jail. Perhaps it is a regretful convict wishing he could turn back the hands of time or a doomed man who knows he is to be taken to Carson City and executed.

This was a rare opportunity, which we enjoyed. However, try as we might, we could not get the guard to admit the place was haunted. "But," he did tell us upon leaving, "the elevators in this building are sometimes weird. When the doors open, I'll hear people chatting away—but they're empty and no one gets out."

We thanked him for the tour and said no more. If he had experienced all this and still wanted to believe that there's no such thing as ghosts, who were we to argue?

Olivia Miller

Yet another ghost is said to roam these hallways. She is Mrs. Olivia Miller, and she died here in a daring escape attempt. Her story begins on the morning of July 16, 1876, when Reno undertaker W. Sanders accompanied Sheriff Jones nine miles north to the Junction House in Poeville (approximately northwest Reno at the foot of Peavine Mountain). Sanders and Sheriff Jones had come to pick up the body of Olivia Miller's husband, Samuel, and take it back to Reno for proper burial.

The dead man lay facedown in the dirt, his head horribly bashed in. The Millers' handsome handyman George DeLong stepped up and told the sheriff how he had been forced to use the axe on his employer. Olivia wrung her hands and wept as DeLong explained that Samuel Miller was a heavy drinker who had come to him drunk and angry. A fight ensued, and Mr. Miller had gotten the worst of it—the very worst of it, by the look of things. While DeLong spoke, Mrs. Miller nodded agreement and sobbed. Sheriff Jones was not impressed.

He was a lawman. He had noticed the looks that Olivia and the handyman had exchanged. Perhaps, he reasoned, Mr. Miller had also noticed the friendliness between these two, and when he complained, he was murdered. The homely wife and the handsome handyman, the sheriff decided, were not telling the truth. He arrested DeLong for murder and Olivia Miller for being his accomplice.

When they got into Reno, there was no question that DeLong was going to jail, but the sheriff wondered what he would do with his female prisoner. She may have stood by and watched her husband being slaughtered, but she should not spend the night in the jail. Olivia Miller would sleep in the district attorney's office. And that's where the trouble started. After one successful escape, she was captured and brought back to the DA's office. That night, she made a second attempt at freedom. This time, she leapt from the second-story office to the ground. Unfortunately, she misjudged the distance from the window ledge to the ground—a fatal mistake. She hit the ground at the wrong angle and died a short time later. She was free. George DeLong was not. He was eventually convicted of manslaughter and spent nine years at the state prison in Carson City.

Thus the *Weekly Nevada State Journal* of September 2, 1876, reported on the death and burial of Mrs. Olivia Miller, "At the altar of sin she sacrificed everything. She sleeps 'unwept, unhonored, and unsung.' Let her fate be a warning. Truly, 'the wages of sin is death.'"

Several years later, the old courthouse was torn down and a larger one built in its stead. This hasn't slowed the ghostly Olivia Miller. She supposedly still haunts the courthouse. However, the specter of a large woman has also been seen on the Riverwalk near the area where she made her fateful leap.

Chapter 2
GAMING GHOSTS AND LEGENDS

IT ALL STARTED HERE

Gambling and games of chance were brought to Nevada by the Chinese who built the railroads. Like all great ideas, gambling was seized upon, and it began in Nevada. Comparing the two cities of Reno and Las Vegas, it's easy to see why people sometimes believe that Las Vegas has always been the most popular city in Nevada—the city where gaming began. But that's not quite true. Long before Las Vegas became the entertainment capital of the world, with its bright lights and glitz, people were rolling the dice and betting the odds on Center Street in downtown Reno. Likewise, Reno was referred to as "Sin City" years before Las Vegas was awarded that appellation.

Nevada is mostly a desert region with very little in the way of natural resources, unless you count gold and silver. While the mining industry is once again active in Nevada, this wasn't the case in 1931. Tourists with money to spend was what the state desperately needed. But first someone needed to come up with a plan to get people here. In 1931, someone did. Phil Tobin, a young assemblyman from Humboldt County, introduced a bill to the Nevada legislature that would legalize gambling in the state. Tobin's bill received wide support and moved quickly through the assembly and the senate. On March 19, 1931, Governor Balzar signed the bill into law. Gambling had finally became a state-sanctioned reality for Nevada.

Las Vegas was still mostly a cowpoke town with a railroad and some palm trees. Obviously, things changed. But before they did, the underworld

Downtown Reno and the arch, circa 1950s. *Author's collection.*

maintained its stronghold on Reno. The overseer of this was George Wingfield. That name might sound familiar to you. Wingfield made his fortune in the gold mines of Goldfield and brought his wealth to Reno. Here he built a mansion and ran a banking empire. At one time, he was the most powerful man in Nevada. The city's top underworld figures, Graham and McKay, were beholden to him and on his payroll. And they ran clubs (what casinos were once called here) illegally and legally on Center Street. Legalities mattered little in early day Reno gaming.

GEORGE WINGFIELD BUILT A MANSION HERE

It's a vacant lot in a prime area of downtown Reno. Facing the Truckee River, the lot has been slotted for a high-rise condo. This is where George Wingfield brought his bride and his Goldfield riches. His bride fled after a few years of marriage and the birth of their two children, and his banks faced ruination. In the process, Wingfield lost some of his power and his wealth. But don't despair—he found true love in the form of his third wife, and theirs was a happily-ever-after romance.

He died here in Reno on Christmas Day 1959. Eventually, the mansion fell into the hands of wealthy strangers and from there into disrepair. Then one day, the mansion mysteriously burned to the ground, and this is where we come in. Some people believe that George Wingfield was involved one way or another in the disappearance of bank clerk Roy Frisch, who was set to testify in federal court. There is also some speculation that Frisch's body was buried in Wingfield's backyard. The lot is fenced and posted with a "No Trespassing" sign. I probably don't need to say it, but I will anyway: "No Trespassing" signs should always to be obeyed. However, there is no sign prohibiting standing on the sidewalk and collecting EVP and using a K-2 meter. On the Reno Ghost Walk, we have had groups attempt to contact both Wingfield and Roy Frisch at this spot. Other than the phrase "Can you help?" nothing else has been collected—yet.

If the proposed high-rise condos are built (and eventually they probably will be), everything will be new and fresh, with great views and right on the river. Oooh-la-la! I shudder at the association fees, and there might just be more shuddering going on within the new building, especially if George Wingfield has staked his ghostly claim on this property in perpetuity. I know he has been seen in the Goldfield Hotel some 250 miles south of here, but who is to say that ghosts can't and don't travel?

There have been sightings of a shadowy figure running across the lot north to south, from the Island Drive side to the Court Street side. Is this George Wingfield as a young man? Possibly. Occasionally someone will get the feeling of being disoriented or frightened while standing on the sidewalk here. That's when it's time to move on, so let's do that.

Ghosts of the El Cortez Hotel

Some employees of the El Cortez believe the place is haunted. There is the sound of high heels clacking across the corridor when no one is in sight. The elevator occasionally runs up to the top floor and down again without any obvious human intervention. There are a lot of strange noises in old buildings, so you can never really tell. The hotel was built in 1931 at the height of Reno's quickie divorce business. With a required six-week residency, all those divorce seekers would need a place to stay.

At the end of the 1940s, the trendsetting Hollywood crowd was divorcing in Las Vegas. The star-struck public followed. This is only one of many changes the old Art Deco–style building has seen in its time at the corner of West Second Street and Arlington Avenue. Its days of chic sophistication

Old postcard shot of the original Reno Arch, circa 1940s. *Author's collection.*

have come and gone. Fifties film star and heartthrob Jeff Chandler might have stayed here back in the day, but don't expect many Hollywood big names to come to the El Cortez Trocadero Lounge and toss back a cold one, unless they are interested in the Nada Dada Motel event.

Are there ghosts at the El Cortez? A week before Halloween 1961, a young couple was in Reno for a conference. During the activities, he danced with another woman more than he should have. Fired with anger and jealousy, the wife stormed to the couple's fourth-floor room at the El Cortez. If he hoped for reconciliation once they were alone, he was disappointed. She was not in the mood to make up.

Lashing out at him, she ran around the room tossing over furniture. She mixed herself a drink, pulled off her eyeglasses and threw them at him on the bed. And then without warning, she ran to the open window and dove out headfirst. She landed facedown on the sidewalk along Arlington Avenue. That's the story he told police, and that's the story he told during a lie detector test. And that explains the lonely woman who has been seen there at the corner of Arlington Avenue and Second Street. She seems to be trying to decide—should she go into the hotel or into the next world?

New owners have begun remodeling the hotel. While this might cause the building's ghostly residents to ramp up their activity, it has also raised some concerns with the Historic Reno Preservation Society (HRPS). This is not a matter of ghosts but of aesthetics and of history. The concern was that original windows and awnings might be altered. According to a February

11, 2015 story written by Jason Hidalgo for the *Reno Gazette Journal*, the El Cortez Hotel is in the Reno City Register of Historic Places. Therefore, the city's Historical Resources Commission would have to approve any work done on the exterior of the building.

Are ghosts easier to deal with than bureaucracy? That would probably be a toss-up. The El Cortez Hotel has been renovated and is today known as the Siegel Suites El Cortez.

JEANS WERE INVENTED HERE

Cowboys wear them. So do socialites, presidents and schoolchildren. Everyone wears jeans. And it so happens that jeans were invented right here in Reno by tailor Jacob Davis.

Jacob Youphes emigrated from Latvia to the United States in 1854. Shortly after arriving, he changed his surname to Davis and set up a small tailor shop in New York. Eventually, he headed west to San Francisco and on to Virginia City. From there, he came to Reno, where he opened his little shop on North Virginia Street. Business was good, and then he met a customer with a serious problem.

The seams and pockets of her hefty husband's work pants kept ripping out, and the repairs were proving costly. She hoped the tailor could make a more durable pair of trousers. Davis's solution was to make the pants of sturdy canvas and to reinforce the seams and pockets with copper rivets. Levi Strauss liked the idea and hired Davis to head up his San Francisco factory. The rest is blue jean history. To commemorate the invention that changed fashion forever, a plaque was placed on North Virginia Street where Davis's little shop stood in 1873.

Today, this is a busy area of Virginia Street. The Knitting Factory nightclub is nearby, and across the street is Harrah's. There is lots of music, people and noise here on the busy weekends. No sightings of Jacob Davis have been reported, but some claim feelings of euphoria and happiness overtake them as they stroll past the plaque commemorating the tailor who changed fashion forever. If you're going to ask me what they were drinking, I'm going to tell you that there is an open container law in Reno. So whatever spirits they were indulging in were consumed in the hotel/casinos and not near the plaque—unless it was during a special event, and then some of the area is seen as a beer garden. Check first.

GHOSTLY SHOWGIRL

Marilyn Monroe filmed her last movie here in Reno. While doing so, she stayed at the Mapes Hotel (we'll get to that story later). So there she was, blond and beautiful. Naturally, or not, a beautiful blond ghost might be assumed to be that of Monroe. But is she the ghostly showgirl who's been seen in some of the downtown casinos? This blonde wears sequins (my kind of ghost) and feathers and has been on occasion also seen on the Wedding Ring Bridge. Now you know the lore, so let's look at some facts.

I believe the showgirl ghost may be that of a victim of the Hotel Golden Fire, one of the worst fires in modern-day Reno. Before the completion of Interstate 80 in the late 1960s, Highway 40 linked the Bay Area to Reno. The highway ran alongside the railroad tracks and, like the tracks, was carved from the side of the Sierra. Even in fair weather, that section of the highway that wound its way around the mountains and over Donner Summit was treacherous. When temperatures dropped in Blue Canyon, the slightest precipitation made the road icy and dangerous.

Reno was a seasonal town. With winter came fewer tourists willing to chance the drive over Donner Summit. Those who did often had problems; the time it took to get from the Bay Area to Reno doubled in the smallest snowstorm. A more severe winter storm could render the road impassable and close it altogether, stranding travelers on the wrong side of the mountain. Experienced visitors who didn't fly in took the bus, the train or waited until spring before coming to Reno.

Spring came early to the Truckee Meadows (another name for the Reno area) in 1962. Highway 40 over Donner was clear; tourists from California took advantage of the mild weather and flocked to town in the middle of the week. At the New Golden Hotel, 143 guests were staying the night.

In the evening, they enjoyed floorshows, and afterward, they strolled downtown Reno, trying their luck in one casino after another. Some adhered to the schedule they lived by at home; most stayed out later than usual. Some broke completely free of the rigid schedules they kept at home and were just making their way back to the comfort of their hotel room as daylight fell across the city on the morning of April 3, 1962. Before the day was out, some of them would become victims of the tragic New Hotel Golden fire.

The Hotel Golden had long been a part of Reno. Tonopah banker Frank Golden Sr. built the hotel in 1906 with money borrowed from George Wingfield. Golden envisioned a hotel that would compete with the elegant

Riverside Hotel. His dream came to fruition, and his hotel was soon known as *the* place to stay.

When Golden died a few years after its completion, the hotel was taken over by the Wingfield family, who also owned the Riverside. After World War II, the ultramodern Mapes Hotel was built. As the tallest building in Nevada, the new hotel threatened other hotels in the city. The Wingfield family sold the Hotel Golden to concentrate on the Riverside.

In the next few years, the Hotel Golden on Center Street would gain a reputation as one of Reno's finest places to stay. During its popularity, the hotel exchanged hands several times. In 1952, the Hotel Golden and the adjoining Bank Club were sold to a Texas millionaire for $6 million. The Texan had a new front door put on his "New Golden" and opened a door between the Golden Casino and the Bank Club. He then leased the Golden Casino and the Bank Club to William Graham. The Golden Bank Club, along with the New Hotel Golden, grew in popularity.

The Texan sold the New Golden to brothers James H. and William Tomerlin two years later. It was still owned by the Tomerlins on the morning of April 3, 1962. James was fishing somewhere off the coast of Mexico; William, who stayed in a swank fourth-floor apartment at the hotel, witnessed the devastation firsthand. Like so many others, he escaped the fire with nothing but the clothes on his back. He stood by and helplessly watched his and his brother's investment go up in flames. The first hint that something was wrong came when a bartender opened a trapdoor to the basement; heavy smoke billowed out. Trained to be ever mindful of the company's cash, a casino manager started clearing money off the tables. He changed his mind when he saw how rapidly the fire was spreading. Unaware that the flames were roaring through the basement directly below the Gay Nineties Bank Club, several gamblers continued dropping nickels into the slot machines.

As thick smoke rose up through the four-story hotel, people panicked. Firemen and policemen ran through the hotel rescuing those who couldn't make it to safety on their own. A guest on the second floor called down to the desk to ask what time it was. She was told, "Get out quick! The building is on fire!"

The fifteen-member cast of Barry Ashton's *Paris Playmates of '62* was staying at the hotel, where they were scheduled to perform for the next several weeks. Instead, their jobs, their clothes and other personal items were all swept away in the flames. Two *Paris Playmates* showgirls staying on the second floor were awakened by the incessant barking of a friend's poodle;

The tragic Hotel Golden fire. Note the Mapes Hotel at left in the photograph. *Author's collection.*

it saved their lives. Carol Maye was not as fortunate. The nineteen-year-old showgirl ran out into the hall, lost her bearings in the blinding smoke and raced back into her room. Hers would be one of the last bodies pulled from the rubble.

Unaware of the danger, dealers at the Bank Club kept right on dealing cards, and people in the Carnival Bar at the Lincoln Alley entrance of the hotel continued drinking. Suddenly, smoke was all around them, and they were forced to leave.

Six people lost their lives in the Hotel Golden Fire. The wrongful death suits totaled over $1 million. Down but not out, the Tomerlin brothers announced plans to build a twenty-four-story hotel on the spot where the Hotel Golden once stood. In 1966, after the completion of a fabulous showroom lounge, bars and casino, the Tomerlins ran out of cash and sold the property to Bill Harrah. Today, Harrah's stands on the site of the old Hotel Golden.

And the beautiful blond ghost continues to walk a lonely path around this area of downtown Reno.

WHITE NOISE

Critics didn't much like the 2005 movie *White Noise*. However, it did well at the box office and brought attention to electronic voice phenomena (EVP.) The possibility that voices of the dead could be recorded captured the public's imagination. Before the movie was released, those who worked in preproduction came to Reno to talk with EVP researchers. It just so happened that my friends were doing a conference on EVP and invited them to take part.

An impromptu investigation of the Nevadan Hotel at 133 Virginia Street downtown was set up, and interviews were conducted. Members of the cleaning staff were quick to tell of ghosts in the hotel. A woman who worked in the ladies' bathroom said that while cleaning the stalls one night, she heard a woman come running into the bathroom and start crying. As she listened, the weeping grew louder and louder.

"Are you alright?" she called out. The crying continued. "Are you okay?" she repeated.

When she received no response, she came out of the stall to see if she could help. To her amazement, she was alone in the bathroom. This happened several times before she learned to ignore the crying woman. According to others, a supervisor committed suicide up in the penthouse. A dark and negative energy seemed to permeate that area. EVP that asked, "Did you want this?" was recorded in this location.

One of the most remarkable things to come from the investigation was a psychic medium's impression of a woman, covered in dust and bricks and crying for help. While it isn't always possible, it is wise to try and validate such impressions. I decided to do just that. After some research, I discovered that on November 21, 1973, a building was being razed when it collapsed and crashed to the sidewalk, killing only one person, a Canadian tourist.

The *Nevada State Journal* of November 22, 1973, reported on the incident:

> *Hilp's Front Falls. A 47 year old Canadian woman was killed and two other persons were injured Wednesday when a 2½ story brick wall column collapsed and tumbled "with a tremendous cracking sound" into the center of Virginia Street.*
>
> *"It looked like an explosion," said Reno Police Sgt. Joe Barrett. "There were bricks and pieces of plywood flying all over the place."*

Oh, yes, the address of the Hilp's building that was being razed? It was 133 Virginia Street. And if this isn't validation, I don't know what is.

WATER, SPIRITS AND OUIJA BOARDS DON'T MIX

With the fame of the Fox sisters, interest in the paranormal, specifically ghosts, swept the country toward the end of the nineteenth century. Everyone wanted to make contact with the dead, and Reno residents were no exception. The following article appeared in the *Daily Nevada State Journal*'s November 14, 1878 issue:

> *The believers in spiritualism in Reno are about to organize a society for the promotion of their creed. They will be called the "Order of Progressive Spiritualists of Reno, Nevada." Should they effect an organization they will hold regular séances, and frequent lectures. There appears to be quite a number of "believers" in town.*

The founder of the Golden Gate Spiritualist Church in San Francisco was Reverend Florence Harwood Becker, who was born in Reno on February 16, 1892. Although she was raised in a strict Methodist home, Becker conversed with spirits from childhood. She often held séances at the church in which spirits would paint beautiful pictures. One of those mysterious paintings is located in a small antique store in Genoa, some forty-six miles south of Reno.

While many people were curious about the afterlife, there was also a staunch segment of the population that strongly opposed the viewpoints of spiritualists. The *Nevada State Journal* of April 28, 1911, carried a story about a hoodoo lecture that was slated for the following week. The article stated, "Dr. George Gilbert Bancroft lecture entertainment on 'Hoodoos' is a banner number. He delivers many telling blows at such 'pet' superstitions as beholding the new moon over your left shoulder, black cats crossing your path, Friday the 13th and a host of others…He has a message for every man, woman and child, and it is a message fraught with meaning and baked up by a world of practical experience and knowledge."

Tickets for the lecture went for fifty cents each. Ah, the good old days. But not so good for the Ouija board, on July 16, 1920, the Mary Pickford hit silent film *Rebecca of Sunnybrook Farm* was showing at the Grand in Reno, Nevada. At the same time, the Reno Power, Light and Water Company wanted to raise utility rates. Opposing the raise were citizens represented by Reno attorney Sardis Summerfield. As the case wore on, briefs were filed and trouble started. One of the attorneys representing the power company filed a brief in which he said he could not understand how Mr. Summerfield had arrived at his conclusion even with the aid of a Ouija board.

His use of the word *Ouija* highly offended Mr. Summerfield, so he quickly filed a motion to strike:

To Messrs. Hoyt, Norcross, Thatcher, Woodburn & Henley and to Messrs. Cheney, Downer, Price and Hawkins and especially to Messrs. Thatcher and Hawkins of said firms. You and each of you will please take notice the undersigned has moved the public service commission of the state of Nevada to strike from the brief filed in and above entitled action by attorney for the Reno Power, Light and Water Company any and all reference therein contained to "ouija board" and any reference whatever therein to the practice of "voodooism" "necromancy" "occultism" "soothsaying" "black arts" "conjury" and similar epithets on the following grounds to-wit.

First that the same are contrary to President Wilson's Fourteen Points.

Second that the same are contrary to the League of Nations.

Third that the same are contrary to the Ten Commandments.

Fourth that the same are slanderous per-se.

An agreement was reached; the offending word was struck from the brief. And as we all know, there is no abating rising water and power bills, even to this day.

Troubles for the Ouija board and its devotees continued in Reno. In an article entitled *Ouija Not Needed,* the April 10, 1922 issue of the *Reno Evening Gazette* reported on a local reverend's thoughts on the Ouija:

"Shall we buy Ouija Boards" was the sermon subject chosen by Rev. Norman W. Pendleton for his morning discourse at the Federated Church yesterday.

"No," was the answer he supplied, and he told his congregation that in twenty-eight years only two mediums had been found who were not frauds, according to the Society Psychical Research.

"Now that brilliant and trustworthy men have obtained messages that indicate the immortality of the soul," he said, "shall we buy ouija boards and indulge in spiritual séances?

"Most emphatically not. Only men of rare training and full scientific equipment are able to detect deceit and fraud. The average man is helpless.

"The great need of the world is the use, the application of known truth; Why look for new 'new revelations' when we fail to use simple scientific truth. Not talks with the dead, but the thunder of truth to the living is our need—prophet who will dare to sound senatorial Washington up alongside 'Woe unto you. Pharisees and stick to the Golden Rule into the coal mines.'"

Ghosts in the Underground Parking Garage

Over the years, I have wondered if the experience was ghostly or some sort of time warp. Regardless, I have never forgotten this story that was told to me several years ago by a co-worker at the old Overland Hotel. This was in the 1970s, and gaming was still very much a Nevada-only activity. Downtown Reno's Virginia Street was lined with hotel/casinos from the Riverside Hotel and Mapes Hotel at the south end to the arch and the railroad tracks at the north end.

The only time that things slowed down was during the winter, when heavy snows on the pass could all but close Interstate 80 and bring business to a standstill. This was long before the drought set in with its warm dry winters. That year's winter was a severe one. Snow was piled high on Donner Summit. Travel into or out of the city was nearly impossible. Stranded tour buses were parked up and down Center Street, while those who'd arrived in them huddled in casino coffee shops awaiting word of departure. Their money was long since spent on the tables, in the slots or at the Keno counter, so wait was all they could do.

With the pass closed, and no customers to serve, casino management eagerly gave early outs (EOs) to its employees. There was nothing to do but

An old postcard photo of the Mapes Hotel, circa 1940–50. *Author's collection.*

stand around and talk with one another anyway, and besides, it was a cost-effective way to keep the bottom line in order.

The person who told me this story remembered that it was so cold that her teeth chattered as she ran the short distance from North Virginia Street to the parking garage on First Street. She recalled:

> *As I entered the garage, I heard people talking in a language I thought might have been Chinese, but I wasn't sure. I looked around but didn't see anyone, so I kept walking toward my car.*
>
> *Just when I started to open the car door, a glint of light caught my eye, and I noticed three old Asian men standing a few feet away from me.*
>
> *It was below freezing, and here they were dressed in what looked like flimsy cotton robes. I was shivering so bad in my parka, I thought, "My God, these old guys are surely going to freeze to death."*
>
> *"Are you lost?" I asked them.*
>
> *They just smiled and nodded at me.*
>
> *I thought they had somehow gotten lost from their tour bus, so I offered to point them toward Center Street where the buses were parked. But they just kept smiling and nodding at me.*
>
> *"Listen you guys, wait here, and I'll find someone who can help you." I jumped in my car and started it up. As soon as the engine was idling normally, the three old men stepped directly in front of the car, and just like that, whoosh, they disappeared!*
>
> *There was nothing sinister about the ghosts. You could even say they were kind of sad.*
>
> *But it was still a long time before I felt good about going in that parking garage by myself after dark.*

Chinese superstition held that the bones of the dead were to be buried in the homeland. Could it be that these were the spirits of Chinese men who happened to be buried nearby? Years later, workmen were excavating near this spot when they uncovered a small Chinese burial site.

Music from Another Time

People who take ghost tours are fun and curious people. They generally love history as well as ghosts. Often they have had their own ghostly experiences, and these they love to share. So it was that during one of Debbie Bender's Bats in the Belfry Ghost Tours of Virginia City, a woman shared her story about a Reno haunting. This occurred, she said, years ago in a former pawnshop, now a gift emporium located at the corner of Virginia and Fourth Streets in downtown Reno.

She was employed at the pawnshop and knew it to be haunted. There was something inexplicable going on inside the building, and it was music. When she came to work in the morning, she knew the building was empty. And yet there would be times that she could clearly hear the sounds of raucous laughter and of roaring '20s music like it was a bar or an old nightclub. The employees all knew the place was haunted, and they used to play a game of sitting in the basement and listening to the ghosts dancing or moving things around upstairs.

Place memory, or residual energy, also includes sound. Apparently, what they were hearing was the audio of a long-ago event without the visual.

Hoodoo Engine No. 2738

The November 27, 1906 Tuesday evening issue of the *Reno Evening Gazette* carried a horrendous story of an accident that took place at Verdi (ten miles west of Reno). The story carried a headline that read, "Engine Derailed by Brakeman's Body." The story continued with its gruesome details of the death of brakeman Jack Webb:

Slipping from the ice covered pilot of the engine on No. 14 at Verdi this morning, Brakeman J.H. Webb, one of the oldest and most reliable employees of the Southern Pacific line, fell in front of the engine, meeting a terrible death beneath the wheels and throwing the heavy engine from the track. The fearful accident was witnessed by Engineer Cronnin, but he was unable to stop his engine before the pony trucks had passed clear over the unfortunate man's body, severing his body from shoulder to thigh, and leaving him a mangled mass of quivering flesh and crushed bones beneath the forward part of the engine. When the monster engine passed over Webb's body the front wheels left the track and sunk into the soft dirt by the side of the rails, allowing the whole weight of the engine to rest upon Brakeman Webb's mangled remains.

As terrible as the story of Engine No. 2738 was, it might help to explain at least one nameless ghost that wanders a certain area in downtown Reno:

A Hoodoo Engine

A peculiar thing about the accident is the fact that engine 2738, which caused the death of Brakeman Webb, is the same engine that ground the life out of an Italian on the Lake Street crossing in this city some months ago. It seems to be a hoodoo engine, and is said to have cost several men their lives.

Train No. 14 was delayed for over an hour by the accident and the remains were brought to this city in the baggage car.

Chapter 3

UNSOLVED

WHERE IS ROY FRISCH?

The Frisch home is on the corner of Court and Arlington Streets. The family still owns it, although the house has long since been converted to office space. Over the years, I have met people who have worked in the building, and they believe it is haunted not by Roy Frisch but by his mother. One woman claimed she had the feeling that she was always being watched by unseen eyes. Given the history of the house, it is not surprising that Mrs. Frisch may haunt it. It is almost as if she has decided to continue waiting for her son, even as a ghost. Is she the only ghost in the house? Someone moves papers, pens and paperclips around, not to mention the unexplained cold drafts and the sound of doors and windows being opened and closed.

Throughout history, people have vanished without a trace, leaving their friends and loved ones to grapple with questions that can never be answered. Roy Frisch's disappearance left his family and the city of Reno baffled—until an Alcatraz convict came forward. Was his explanation the truth?

The untimely death of Governor Fred Balzar in Carson City the day before had cast a pall across the state. But Mrs. Frisch's bridge party would be held as planned. She and her daughters had spent the day preparing for the evening's activities. Roy Frisch wanted no part of that. Instead, he would go see *Gallant Lady*, a new movie showing at the Majestic Theater, rather than suffer through the party.

The Frisch house. *Photo by Bill Oberding.*

"I'm going to a show. I'll be home early," Roy Frisch said, walking out the front door of the home he shared with his widowed mother and two sisters on the corner of Court and Belmont (now Arlington) Streets.

It was March 22, 1934, 7:45 p.m. He walked out onto the sidewalk. It was a nice night; he would leave his late-model car parked in the garage. Stopping just long enough to adjust his gray fedora, he glanced briefly back at his home before turning and walking east on Court Street. If he hurried, he would be at the Majestic Theater in time to see the newsreel.

He was scheduled to leave for New York early the next morning. His testimony had already resulted in four convictions, and now he was under subpoena to testify in federal court against his former employers, James McKay and Bill Graham. Frisch was a quiet man; any apprehension he may have felt concerning his appearance in federal court was kept from those closest to him.

Forty-five-year-old Frisch had served as a city councilman and county assessor. He had fought in World War I and was one of Reno's upstanding citizens. His father, Charles Jacob, had come from Switzerland as a teenager to work on the Comstock; later, he settled in Reno and operated the Pyramid

House on the corner of Commercial Row and Lake Street. As he walked, Roy may have thought of his father, dead seven years now. Testifying against McKay and Graham was a big responsibility, one his father would have approved of. As a cashier at the Riverside Bank, he had inadvertently found himself working for the two Reno underworld figures. He didn't like their haphazard way of doing business and had even pointed out to them that some of their transactions were questionable. His testimony was necessary to secure a conviction. He had no problem doing what he knew was right.

At the Majestic Theater, he chose a seat in the loge and stared at the screen intently. Later, an usher remembered seeing Frisch there in the loge, engrossed in the film. When the movie was over, Frisch and a friend walked down Virginia Street together. At Court Street, they went their separate ways. Roy turned and walked west along Court Street. Halfway between his home and the sheriff's office, he encountered another friend. According to the man, it was 10:15 p.m. when they stopped to chat. The conversation was brief; they said their goodbyes and parted company. It was the last time anyone other than his killer would see Roy Frisch alive.

When the bridge party ended shortly before 2:00 a.m., Roy had still not returned home. Mrs. Frisch saw her last guest off and looked in at her son's bedroom at half past two o'clock. The coverlet on his bed was still neat and unturned. When he did return, Roy would need to see in order to fit his key in the lock, so she left the porch light on for him. It was still shining when she woke the next morning.

She called everyone she could think of to ask if they'd heard from Roy. No one had. Mrs. Frisch's motherly concern turned to fear as the hours passed. This was not like her son. If he could, he would surely have contacted her by now. Still, she clung to hope.

Since Roy Frisch was under federal subpoena, his disappearance looked suspicious from the start. His description was teletyped across the country. Two days later, there was still no sign of Frisch. Preparations were underway at the Civic Center in Reno for the Sunday afternoon funeral of Governor Fred Balzar. But no one had forgotten Roy Frisch. While police and sheriff's deputies chased leads, members of the American Legion and Elks Club came forward and offered their assistance in the quest. Frisch was a member of both organizations.

Sheriff Russell Trathen called in 120 Nevada National Guardsmen to help in the search for the missing man. Everyone had a theory about his fate; he was a victim of amnesia or had been kidnapped for ransom. The most popular theory was that Frisch had been abducted and, in the parlance of the day, "taken for a ride" in retaliation for his testimony that sent four men to prison for defrauding an elderly hotelkeeper out of his $140,000 life savings. Then, too, without Frisch's testimony, the government's case against McKay and Graham was severely weakened.

Roy Frisch had recently been appointed assistant to bank receiver Leo F. Schmitt, who oversaw several of the state's recently closed banks. Frisch's books and paperwork from the Riverside Bank were examined closely. Everything was in order. Those who knew him best expected nothing less. The missing man was a fine citizen who didn't smoke, drink or gamble.

Three days after Frisch's disappearance, Reno Police chief J.M. Kirkley asked federal investigators to help in the case. Washoe County commissioners unanimously approved a resolution and authorized the sheriff to offer rewards totaling $1,000 for information on Frisch's whereabouts. The resolution read:

> *Whereas: This community has been shocked by the mysterious disappearance of one of its outstanding citizens, Roy J. Frisch and,*
>
> *Whereas the circumstances surrounding the strange and unaccounted for disappearance of said Roy J. Frisch have caused the citizens of Washoe county great concern and,*
>
> *Whereas an affidavit has been filed with said board to the effect that the said Roy J. Frisch has been the victim of foul play and,*
>
> *Whereas the county commissioners believe it to be to the best interests of the people of this county that the mystery be solved at the earliest possible date and to that end that the citizens be interested in making search for said Roy J. Frisch.*
>
> *Now therefore be it resolved that the county commissioners offer a reward of five hundred ($500) dollars to anyone who produces the body of said Roy J. Frisch, and be it further resolved that a reward of five hundred ($500) dollars be offered for the arrest and safe delivery of any perpetrator or perpetrators of any crime in connection with the unsolved disappearance of said Roy J. Frisch.*

The reward was never collected. Frisch's disappearance might have been one of opportunity. With the news of Govern Balzar's unexpected death, those who wanted Roy Frisch out of the way might have sprang into action, thinking that attention would be diverted from the Frisch mystery by the funeral of Governor Balzar. But they were wrong. Acting governor Morley Griswold added his concerns for solving the case with the following statement.

Realizing that this is the first mysterious disappearance of one of our leading citizens, I desire to cooperate to the fullest extent. There is no provision in law known to me or to Gray Mashburn, Attorney General, whereby rewards may be offered.

However, I pledge the executive department at this time to use every effort to secure sufficient monies from the state to meet and match the reward offered by the county commissioners of Washoe County. I feel it my duty and I will use all of the resources of the state of Nevada to apprehend and to bring to justice anyone who may be responsible for the disappearance of, or to find, an esteemed citizen who has disappeared.

Full instructions have been given for a full and thorough investigation to ascertain the true facts.

Searchers combed the area around Peavine Mountain and the abandoned cabins along the Truckee River and even went so far as to drag the river bottom with grappling hooks. Nothing turned up—no clues and no body. Days slipped into weeks, and still there was no sign of the missing man.

Two months after Roy Frisch vanished, a new indictment was issued in the United States District Court against James McKay and William Graham; the defendants were charged with three, instead of the original two, counts of mail fraud. Free on $10,000 bail each, McKay and Graham pleaded not guilty.

The trial proceeded in July as scheduled. Taking Frisch's place as a principal witness was J.M Fuetsch, a former co-worker in the defunct Riverside Bank. On the witness stand, Fuetsch said of Frisch, "He told me he would rather be dead than get mixed up in this thing. But on the night he disappeared, he seemed to be in the best spirits I ever saw him. He had talked with me about what he intended to do the next day and seemed to have no intention of committing suicide or disappearing…It is my opinion that he was taken for a ride."

It was an opinion many shared. A year after Roy Frisch went missing, two Renoites stood trial in San Francisco Federal Court for conspiring to harbor fugitive Lester Gillis, aka Baby Face Nelson, while he resided in Reno. The two people involved knew him only as Jimmy Burnell and claimed they had no knowledge of the gangster's true identity, but they acknowledged that he had a volatile temper.

They had seen him furiously pacing up and down a section of the old Geiger Grade on the way to Virginia City, with a machine gun strapped to his shoulder. It seemed that federal agents were wise to him and watching the garage where his car was parked; Nelson had desperately tried to talk his partner into going into the garage with machine guns blazing.

The prosecutor asked, "Was the person you knew as Jimmy Burnell a chauffeur to William Graham?"

"Yes, he was," the defendants answered.

Later, J. Edgar Hoover reported that John Paul Chase, an Alcatraz inmate who was serving time for the murder of two FBI agents, had come forward and admitted to witnessing the murder of Roy Frisch by Baby Face Nelson. According to Chase, he and Nelson came to Reno on March 20. Two nights later, they were driving through town when they happened upon Frisch walking alone. Nelson jumped out of the car, knocked him out with the butt of his gun and dragged him into the car.

They then drove to a Reno garage, where the unconscious Frisch was transferred to another car and shot in the head. His body was then driven some 150 miles from Reno and dumped down an abandoned mine shaft. Authorities believed this location was probably somewhere around Hawthorne, where the Nelson gang was known to have hidden out. A search of the area turned up nothing. Other locations that have been suggested for the body dump were Spanish Springs and an area between Virginia City and Silver City.

By 1938, Roy Frisch had been gone four years. After two trials and two deadlocked juries, the government proceeded with its third mail fraud case against James McKay and William Graham. John Paul Chase was summoned to New York to give testimony concerning the murder of Roy Frisch, the government's principal witness. Because of the danger involved in transporting a criminal of Chase's standing, special precaution was taken in that transfer. After all the trouble, he was not called as a witness.

On February 12, 1939, James McKay and William Graham were convicted of mail fraud and of operating a swindling ring. They were ordered to pay $11,000 each in fines and were sentenced to nine years in Leavenworth Federal Penitentiary.

Seven years after her son's disappearance, Mrs. Frisch petitioned the district court to have him legally declared dead. That order was entered by Judge Curler on July 15, 1941.

McKay and Graham were paroled four years later, in October 1945. Reno was their home, and they returned here after having served six years of their sentences. Money always talks. In this case, it seemed to be screaming. In 1950, McKay and Graham were given full pardons by President Harry S. Truman, thanks to Nevada senator Pat McCarran, whose Reno home was, incidentally, located across the street from the Frisch family home. How this turn of events must have made Mrs. Frisch feel, we can only imagine.

So what did happen to Roy Frisch? Every few years, someone comes forward with a new theory. So far there is nothing to prove these theories. My guess (or theory, if you prefer) is that he was taken out to a deserted area north of town (the present Spanish Springs). There, a deep hole was waiting. He was shot and tossed in it. Did I mention that George Wingfield owned a ranch and much land out there?

Who Shot Fitz?

Another Reno mystery that endures took place nearly two decades after the disappearance of Roy Frisch. It's the shooting of Lincoln Fitzgerald on November 19, 1949. It was an autumn night. A breeze whispered across treetops, and the full moon dropped behind the Sierra, leaving the midnight sky to the myriad stars that sparkled across it. Lincoln Fitzgerald glanced at his watch; there was still a good half hour before his shift started at the Nevada Club. He had no intentions of being late. He would be on time, even though it didn't matter what time he arrived. He answered to no one. He was the owner of the popular downtown gambling club.

He stepped out the back door and walked over to the garage. All the homes along Mark Twain Avenue were dark; the neighbors had long since called it a night. They didn't work the late shift like he did. But it all evened out—in the morning while he slept warm and toasty, the day shifters would be warming up their cars.

His breath formed puffs in the cold night air as he slowly raised the garage door. Suddenly, a shotgun blast tore through the silence. Lincoln Fitzgerald fell where he stood; two more shots rang out in quick succession.

Meta Fitzgerald dropped her hairbrush and ran for the door.

"What happened? What happened?" she screamed, racing toward her husband.

She stopped and stared at the dark puddle of blood that flowed from his wounds. Ever so gently, she bent and touched her husband's arm. "You're gonna be all right, Fitz," she whispered.

Neighbors, awakened by the commotion, came running in housecoats and slippers. Nothing like this had ever happened in their posh Newlands

The Commercial Row area of downtown, circa 1940s. *Author's collection.*

Manor neighborhood of respectable families, stately brick mansions and tall pine trees. What could they do to help?

"My husband's been shot," Meta told those who crept closer.

One of those who stood in the driveway with Meta that night was Miles Pike, a United States attorney who lived two doors away. Pike took one look at Fitz and ran back into his own home for a blanket and a towel. The injured man would be made as comfortable as possible.

Minutes later, a squad car pulled up to the home on 123 Mark Twain Avenue, and two policemen jumped out. The yellow glow of flashlights whirled around the front yard, then the backyard and finally the alley behind the Fitzgerald home. There was nothing. The shooter could be drinking a celebratory whiskey at a Center Street bar, chuckling to himself in a motel room far out on Virginia Street, describing the job over the telephone to his bosses or hotfooting it out of town. Whoever he was, he was long gone. Meta knew that much, even as the police officers searched the yard.

In the distance, the plaintive wail of an ambulance's siren pierced through the night's calm. Meta willed its driver to hurry, please hurry…

What were the odds for Fitz's survival? Even at fifty-seven years old, he was strong and healthy, and this gave him a fighting chance. While police investigated the attempted murder of Lincoln Fitzgerald, savvy Renoites whispered that Fitz's past had finally caught up with him. Perhaps it had.

Shortly after World War II, the State of Michigan began cleaning up its illegal gambling problem. This left partners Lincoln Fitzgerald and Dan Sullivan, who were operating a lucrative gambling club on the outskirts of Detroit, scrambling for a more acceptable locale. The choice was simple. Nevada was the only state in the nation where gambling was legal. Why worry about the law when you could operate within it—and still make a profit? In 1945, they came to Reno and opened the Nevada Club. It seemed the perfect solution for the men who'd figured so prominently in Michigan gambling. But their troubles were far from over. Within a year, Michigan charged Lincoln Fitzgerald and Dan Sullivan with conspiracy to violate Michigan's anti-gambling laws, bribing public officials and being fugitives from justice. In asking for the pair's extradition, Michigan contended they had fled the state solely to avoid prosecution.

Fitzgerald and Sullivan fought the extradition, claiming they were the victims of "political persecution." Nevada governor Vail Pittman, who presided over the extradition hearing, refused to extradite the two Reno businessmen. He believed a one-man grand jury was unconstitutional and didn't adhere to American concepts of justice. Pittman did state, however, "When a common law grand jury indictment is returned by Michigan, the extradition of the defendants will be immediately effected."

After a third extradition request and much legal maneuvering, Fitzgerald and Sullivan were returned to Michigan to stand trial on charges of conspiracy to evade Michigan's anti-gambling laws (the bribery charges were dropped). Each man was fined $700 plus court fees. Their fees were the highest court fees ever assessed by a Michigan court at that time: Sullivan's fees amounted to $33,000, and Fitzgerald's were $18,000.

Fitzgerald's injuries were extensive. He had lost a lot of blood. The first shot from the sawed-off twelve-gauge shotgun had damaged his liver, perforated his lung and severed his spinal cord. But he was lucky; had that first shot not knocked him off his feet, Fitz would be starring in a funeral. While he lay fighting for his life in Washoe Hospital, the rumors continued. The shooting had been a failed mob hit. It was revenge for something in his Michigan past. The notorious Purple Gang was somehow involved. Rumor was Fitzgerald had taken a lot of his former bosses' cash with him when he went to Nevada. As you might expect, they didn't take kindly to this.

Reno police called the shooting a "midnight alley ambush" and believed the shooter had been very close to his target. An outspoken police officer predicted that the case would end up like that of Bugsy Siegel. He was right on the mark. Bugsy's assailant had taken aim, shot to kill and then disappeared into the night. So had Lincoln Fitzgerald's.

The only difference was that the hit on Bugsy was successful while that of Lincoln Fitzgerald was not. The case was never solved. One reason, according to rumors that still persist, was that Lincoln Fitzgerald himself asked the police to stop all investigation of the incident. After five months, Lincoln Fitzgerald was finally able to leave the hospital. As a result of his injuries, he would walk with a limp the rest of his life. He was not a stupid man. He would never again stay at the home on Mark Twain Drive. Becoming reclusive, Fitzgerald moved into a special room at the Nevada Club and rarely left the building. When he did, it was always in the company of a burly bodyguard.

Lincoln Fitzgerald might have been elderly, but he had a reputation among many of the female employees. Some of them swore that while interviewing them he had asked the most blatantly sexist and personal questions imaginable. Those who needed the job answered and forgot about it. Those who didn't walked out of the interview room. He died in 1981, five years after opening Fitzgerald's, his new hotel/casino. But there were rumors of his smiling apparition having appeared throughout the casino, especially in the counting room. Wouldn't this be like him to flout the Nevada Gaming Commission rule that states no casino owner is permitted into his or her establishment's counting room? Of course, the rules may not apply when said owner is a ghost.

One question remains to this day: who shot Fitz?

WHAT BECAME OF GERALD LAYNE?

Throughout history, there have been cases of someone disappearing without a trace. When someone just vanishes, it leaves questions that may never be answered. Was it a voluntary absence or something more sinister? With thirty-five-year-old Gerald Layne, some said he was heavily in debt to the wrong people and wanted to make a fresh start. Then, too, there are those who insist the man would never have vanished like that. But he did.

On January 6, 1961, the Riverside Hotel's acting general manager Gerald Layne was awaiting approval of his gaming license by the Nevada Gaming Control Board. Approval would place him at the gambling zenith. He would own 5 percent of the swank Riverside Hotel and assume the job of general manager on a permanent basis.

Riverside Hotel, circa 1950–60. *Author's collection.*

Shortly before the Nevada Gaming Control Board reached its decision, Layne, an avid card player, set out with $15,000 for a high stakes card game in Placerville. He was never seen or heard from since. Neither were the one-and-a-quarter-carat diamond ring and jade cufflinks he was wearing. The *Reno Evening Gazette* of Monday, January 9, 1961, reported:

> *An intensive land and air search was launched this morning by police and Air Force personnel for a Reno casino executive who vanished Friday enroute to Placerville, Calif., to participate in a "high stakes" card game. He was carrying several thousands of dollars police were told. Reported as missing is Gerald E. Layne, 35 year-old casino manager at the Riverside Hotel and former executive at the New Frontier Casino in Las Vegas. Loyal Morrow, 41, uncle of the missing man, who is also a Riverside Casino employee, said Layne left Reno Friday in a 1960, white American-made car. He said Layne was scheduled to participate in a card game with professional gamblers at request of a promoter friend, Glen Lucas, of Las Vegas. Morrow said he talked with Lucas later and Layne had never arrived. The game was called off. Las Vegas police told Reno authorities that Lucas later returned to southern Nevada but was not there Monday morning. They believed he was driving towards Mexico. Police are attempting to locate Lucas for further details. Reno police said a helicopter left Stead Air Force*

Base at 10:30 a.m. today to search the highways between Reno, Lake Tahoe and Placerville, Calif., the route Layne would probably have taken. Layne and his uncle worked at the New Frontier in Las Vegas until late in 1960 when the Riverside was purchased by Las Vegas showman Bill Miller. Layne was hired by Miller as casino manager. Morrow went to work for his nephew. For several years, Layne and Morrow lived in Rifle, Colo., but left there for Las Vegas in 1939. Morrow said Layne was a skilled poker player who for several years made his living with cards. The missing casino manager is described as 5'10" in height and weighing about 180 pounds. He has black hair and dark eyes. When last seen he was wearing a brown suit, and a white shirt with jade cuff links at the sleeves.

Morrow said he agreed with police in the possibility of foul play. Layne was scheduled to return to duty Friday at midnight.

The next day, the *Reno Evening Gazette* of January 10, 1961, reported the following:

OFFICIALS FIND MISSING CASINO MAN'S VEHICLE
The search for a Reno casino manager who disappeared Friday while enroute to Placerville, Calif. with several thousand dollars, has centered in the Lake Tahoe area, Frank Garske, Reno police captain disclosed, today. The search for Gerald E. Layne narrowed Monday night upon the discovery of Layne's 1960 model car in the Harrah's Club parking lot at the lake. Layne was scheduled to leave Reno Friday for a "high stakes" card game in Placerville, Calif. He was slated to return to work at the casino Friday night. His Uncle, Loyal Morrow, reported Layne failed to appear at the hotel by late Sunday night. Morrow said he talked to a Las Vegas promoter, Glen Lucas, who had arranged the card game. Lucas reportedly told Morrow that Layne had not appeared in Placerville and the card game was "called off." Las Vegas police reported Lucas resumed to that area Saturday but left again Sunday. His destination was not determined but it may have been to the Reno area, Southern Nevada investigators said Tuesday, Douglas County, officials reported they found nothing in Layne's white colored car but they quickly added that they did not make thorough examination. They were awaiting arrival of specialists from Reno. Capt. Garske said the car was being held at the Sheriff's substation at Zephyr Cove. A helicopter from Stead Air Force Base covered the routes which Layne would have taken to the card game but failed to find the auto Monday. Layne, a former executive at the New Frontier Casino in Las Vegas was hired recently by

Riverside Hotel man Bill Miller as casino operator. Morrow, 41, was hired by Layne to work in the casino. Layne and Morrow worked together in Rifle, Colo., before residing in Las Vegas.

Five days later, the Nevada Gaming Control board denied the missing man's gaming license application. The January 14, 1961 issue of the *Reno Evening Gazette* reported:

BOARD OUSTS MISSING RENO GAME EXECUTIVE
Gerald Layne, missing Reno gaming executive, was ousted from Nevada's gambling industry Friday by the state Gaming Control Board because of a police record. The onetime Rifle, Colo., pool hall owner was refused five percent of the Riverside casino in Reno and also ruled ineligible to continue as its manager.

FEAR FOUL PLAY
Layne, formerly a Las Vegas gambler, has been missing for one week despite a search by Reno police and other law enforcement agencies who fear foul play. He vanished Jan. 6 carrying about $15,000 in cash to a private poker game in Placerville, Calif, police believe he never reached Placerville and they found his car at Lake Tahoe. The board took its action after reading into the record evidence the 32-year-old manager of one of Reno's plushest gambling clubs was arrested two years ago in Tulsa, Okla., with a carload of crooked cards and dice and a loaded pistol. The board took no action on co-applicant for a five per cent [sic] Riverside interest, Portland, Ore., insurance man Frank Cundari. Although Cundari was to have loaned Layne $17,000 towards his stock purchase, the board witheld [sic] recommendation on his application solely because it has not yet received complete information on the changing corporate structure of the big hotel-casino now operated by showman Bill Miller.

POLICE RECORDS
The denial recommendation for Layne was based on police records and court action taken in Tulsa in May, 1959, when the young gambler allegedly crashed an oilmen's party in a large hotel and tried to drum up an illegal card game. Police reports indicate his belongings included a .22 caliber pistol, numerous pairs of loaded dice and decks of marked cards, and an assortment of card-marking paraphernalia. He was fined a total of $165 for vagrancy, drunkenness, resisting arrest, possession of a concealed

weapon and possession of gambling equipment. Board Chairman Ray J. Ahbaticchio Jr. ordered his agents to check the status of two Las Vegas dealers arrested in Tulsa at the same time as Layne. They were identified as Harold Pearson and Bill Bickel. The gaming board revealed that Layne appeared before it at its own request Dec. 6 to "give his side" to the Tulsa arrest. Layne's version was at complete odds with the one revealed by police files. Questioning by Ahbaticchio of chief enforcement agent Robert Moore disclosed only a casual investigation was made of Layne's background in 1956, when he was licensed for a brief period at the Alibi Club in Henderson, but that no question of cheating had ever been raised concerning him as a Nevada licensee or dealer.

No Jurisdiction

Moore told Ahbaticchio no specific investigation had been made of Layne's disappearance because "that is outside of the board's jurisdiction." Abbaticchio's only reference to the disappearance was a terse statement that: "The board looks with disfavor on licensees or applicants going outside Nevada to participate in illegal gambling." The motion to recommend denial of the application was made by board member Ned Turner. The action does not necessarily bar Layne from employment in Nevada gambling. Meanwhile, Reno police said that Las Vegas promoter Glen Lucas was unable to furnish any additional information into the disappearance of the casino manager. Assistant Police Chief William Brodhead said Las Vegas authorities questioned Lucas Friday. He admitted setting up the poker game in Placerville, Calif., and inviting Layne. Lucas told police that when Layne did not show up he phoned the hotel and asked about him. After another wait, he said he called off the poker game and returned to Las Vegas. From there he went to Mexico and returned to Las Vegas. Lucas was arraigned in Justice Court Friday on a bad check warrant issued in Oregon. Bail was set at $500 cash or $1,000 in property. He refused to waive extradition.

Makes Statement

Miller made this formal statement last night after learning the Nevada Gaming Control Board had rejected Layne's application for a five percent interest on the license: "During the period that I have known Gerald Layne I have never had occasion to do anything but admire him. I have been advised that the Nevada Gaming Control Board has uncovered certain evidence pertaining to his activities in Tulsa, Okla. in a time before I knew him.

Gerald never saw fit to acquaint me with those activities, nor was I aware of them when I considered taking him in to my operation at the Riverside Hotel. I don't feel that it would be fair to comment on these matters at this time when the man concerned is not available to answer or defend himself. I am impressed with the thoroughness of the investigation conducted by the Gaming Control Board, and wish to commend them on their efficiency. Their action bears out what I have always intended: that with effective supervision, undesirables or improper personnel will find it difficult, if impossible at all, to infiltrate the gambling business in Nevada."

So this didn't necessarily bar Gerald Layne from a job in the gaming industry. It seemed doubtful he would ever need a job again. And as they always do in such cases, rumors flew. But like the disappearance of Roy Frisch decades prior, the mystery surrounding the fate of Gerald Layne has never been solved. Might we assume that Layne has returned to the Riverside Artist Lofts to reclaim his position as general manager? Is he responsible for the footsteps and heavy thuds that are heard at all hours of the day and night in the artist loft? I'm betting he is.

ALF DOTEN'S GHOST

Alfred Doten came to northern Nevada in 1863. A journalist by trade, Doten worked as a carpenter in Como (near Dayton) only a short while before moving to the more exciting Comstock. A prolific writer, Alf Doten wrote for both the *Territorial Enterprise* and the *Gold Hill Evening News,* of which he was owner/editor writer. The journals he kept during this period of his life are a valuable resource to historians and others interested in early Northern Nevada history, particularly that of Virginia City and Gold Hill.

A man of varied interests and talents, he filled his journals with odd and lurid goings-on. Occasionally he wrote of encounters with the paranormal while using a contraption known as "the dial," a precursor to the Ouija board.

On a family Christmas visit to Reno in 1890, Doten found the town bustling with excitement over the phantom of a woman that was appearing on the Westside. Ever in search of a byline and a check, Doten wrote of the ghostly apparition for that city's *Daily Nevada State Journal.*

According to Doten, it all happened when a woman, who was headed home from the Reno Opera House, happened upon the ghostly figure of a woman standing near the Congregational church. Some thought the phantom was nothing more than a college boy's prank.

Perhaps, but the apparition appeared in mourning black, leading some to believe that she was the ghost of a woman who had committed suicide over the tragic loss of her husband.

Doten's article went on to tell of how a young man, who wanted to impress a certain young lady with his bravery, chased the ghost a few blocks. Finally, when he was within reach of the ghost, it vanished before his eyes. The identity of the ghost of the mourning woman has never been revealed. Maybe this was nothing more than a prank. But if it wasn't, might the phantom woman still haunt this area of Reno?

THE HAUNTED PEDERCINI HOUSE

Nowadays, there are so many ghost-hunting groups that you won't have to look far to have someone come and investigate your house if you suspect there are ghosts about. But in the early days of the twentieth century, it was a different matter. Two weeks before the San Francisco Earthquake struck that city, the *Daily Nevada State Journal* of Thursday, April 5, 1906, carried the story of a haunted house, stating, "GHOST DECLARED TO HAUNT A HOME. Reno is said to be harboring a real 'spook' and families live in fear. Priest called to exorcise the spirit. Pedercini's residence scene of alleged visits—clanking chains and trembling dishes."

The story went on:

> Reno has a haunted house. It is located at the corner of Second and West Street and is occupied by G. Pedercini family, who moved to Reno one week ago from Truckee[;] Mrs. Martin, mother of Mrs. Pedercini[;] and B.L. Hunt, who owns the house.
>
> The "ghost" seems to have a strange habit of moving pieces of furniture, and dishes about the room. A strange noise resembling the clanking of chains are also heard and rather hideous sounds all of which have so preyed upon the minds of the occupants of the house, with the exception of Hunt, that they are distracted over the unexplainable chain of strange and terrifying events.
>
> As a last resource the services of Father Tubman were sought. Yesterday morning and again last night he "exorcised the spirit" at the haunted house

and it is believed by the occupants of the house that this will dispel the actions of the "spook."

In speaking of the strange affair yesterday, Mrs. Pedercini said, "Every night since we moved to this house from Truckee our lives have been made miserable by strange noises and actions of some unseen hand or power. The events occur at about the same time each evening between 7 and 9 o'clock, and are confined to the kitchen and pantry. Usually they only last a few minutes, but last Sunday night the strange noises continued for the period of about half an hour. On that evening the dishes which we used for the evening meal jumped from the table to the floor and dishes in the cupboard were overturned by the action of some hidden power. We are all thoroughly frightened at the strange events and shall certainly change our place of residence if the actions of the priest do not have any effect on the visits of the "ghost."

Father Tubman, when approached about the matter yesterday, admitted that he had been called to the home of the Pedercini's [sic] and said he tried to persuade them that there could be no such trouble as they imagined, and that the fancied work of the spook was not really a fact. On their insistence they did not imagine these things, he did what he could to finally allay their fears.

Sometimes you've just got to put some distance between yourself and a ghost. In the end, the Pedercinis did just that. They packed up and moved to nearby Sparks. The ghost apparently didn't follow. Two days after the article appeared, the Pedercinis' landlord B.L. Hunt hinted that he was responsible for the ghostly goings on in the house because he wanted the Pedercinis to move. Was the house haunted by a ghost or by a mean-spirited landlord?

If you're curious, a location that is very near where the Pedercinis' haunted house once stood is presently near the site of the West Second Street Bar in downtown Reno. My friend Debbie Bender told me that the place is said to be haunted and that local groups have investigated it. They say it's very active. Apparently, some of Reno's early tunnels are beneath the bar, and it is from here that the ghostly activity stems.

Chapter 4

MARRIAGE, DIVORCE AND THE LEGENDS

KISSING A COURTHOUSE PILLAR

The second Washoe County Courthouse was designed by Frederick De Longchamps, one of Nevada's preeminent architects. Larger and more elaborate than the first courthouse, the new courthouse was built in 1911. The total construction cost of the courthouse was $250,000. That's less than the median price of a home in the Reno area today. Okay, so that was a century ago—what about those ghosts said to roam the hallowed halls? There are a few. One of them is an elderly judge who fell down a flight of stairs and passed from this life to the next without handing down a ruling. Others are mostly those who lived and died on the wrong side of the law. We'll catch up with these miscreants a bit later.

While all courthouses are synonymous with justice, Reno's would also become famous for divorce, especially for all the celebrities of that era who came here seeking divorces. In 1931, two years before Prohibition was repealed, Nevada legalized gambling once and for all, but gambling revenue was not enough to fill the state's coffers. Once Arkansas reduced its waiting period for a divorce down to six months, the race was on. Nevada would do Arkansas one better. Not wanting to be left behind in the lucrative divorce business, the state introduced its six-week residency requirements soon afterward, in 1934.

The other forty-seven states were scandalized. So be it—nightlife fun, gambling and quickie divorces would bring money to Nevada and set it

An old postcard depicts the Washoe County Courthouse shortly after it was built in 1911. *Author's collection.*

apart. The rich and the famous were the first to see the advantages. Every Hollywood star wanting out of an old marriage and into a new one headed for Reno. By train and plane and car, they came.

These lightning-speed divorces garnered worldwide attention for the Biggest Little City in the World. By the early 1940s, Reno was considered the Divorce Capital of the World—in spite of the fact that marriages here far outnumbered divorces. In 1943, 5,816 divorce decrees were granted in Washoe County; that same year, 15,811 marriage licenses were issued. Somehow the idea of a spur-of-the-moment wedding wasn't nearly as scandalous as the ability to shed one's mate at the speed of light.

As you might suspect, Reno has its superstitions, and no one is more susceptible to a superstition than the newly divorced. Hence, the kissing of a pillar. Some may argue it was nothing but a publicity stunt. Tell that to the women, and perhaps men, who, after gaining their freedom, went out the front doors of the courthouse, leaned over and kissed one of its pillars. This was supposed to bring good luck to the kisser in his or her next matrimonial adventure. It was such a popular custom that kissing the pillar was featured on the front cover of the June 21, 1937 issue of *Life* magazine.

This brings us to another Reno "did she or didn't she" debate. Some of Marilyn Monroe's scenes from the movie *The Misfits* were filmed at the front door of the Washoe County Courthouse. In the movie, she did not kiss a pillar. Nor did she do this after shooting (maybe she should have). But there are those who still insist that she did indeed kiss one of the pillars. The story of Monroe's alleged kissing of the pillar is so old that the teenage boys who raced down to the courthouse in search of the blonde's lip prints are now grandfathers.

MARILYN MONROE AND *THE MISFITS*

Talk about traveling ghosts. Marilyn Monroe died in Brentwood, California, yet her ghost has been seen all over the country. Occasionally, she is spotted here in Reno, Nevada. This is understandable. Her last movie was filmed here, and she seemed to enjoy her time here.

In July 1960, all of Reno was excited about the prospect of movie stars coming to town for the filming of a major motion picture. Other movies had been made in and around Reno, and stars still came for their divorces. They snuck into town; did their six-week residencies at the Riverside, the Mapes or some out-of-the-way dude ranch; and then dashed away, ready to try their luck with love and marriage once again.

This time, the stars in town included Marilyn Monroe and leading man Clark Gable. It didn't get any better than that. The eyes of the city fathers glistened with anticipation of all that publicity. Reno was on the map. Never had so much glamour or world attention been thrust on the Biggest Little City.

Gable was already in town and doing scenes that didn't require his co-star. Marilyn Monroe arrived at the Reno Airport a few days into shooting. A crowd of nearly three hundred adoring fans waited under the scorching Nevada summer sun for her. Never mind that it would take nearly an hour for her to disembark the plane. File it under let them wait…and wait.

Among the dignitaries in attendance were Reno's mayor and the wife and daughter of Nevada governor Grant Sawyer. Monroe played no favorites. She made them all wait. She must look her best. Her clothes had to be changed and her hair just so before she could greet her fans. Nearly an hour after landing, the plane's door opened and out she stepped. Strolling across the tarmac, she waved to her cheering fans. A broad smile crossed her face as the star was led first to the mayor, who presented her with the keys to the city, and then to Nevada's first lady. Smiling sweetly, Monroe accepted a bouquet from the governor's teenage daughter, Gail, and then made her way to an awaiting car.

No one in the crowd on that dry desert afternoon could have known that *The Misfits* would be her last film. Within a year, some of those who cheered for the beautiful blond star that day would mourn her death. While in Reno, Monroe's troubles escalated. Co-star Clark Gable considered himself a professional; her lack of professionalism appalled him. Director John Houston lost patience with her and her habit of arriving on the set at least two hours late. She was moody and appeared to be in a drug-induced stupor at times. Some observers thought she looked haggard. She was, after all, pushing forty—not a good age for Hollywood stars, as all those starlets twenty years younger kept on coming.

Her marriage to playwright Arthur Miller was crumbling, and their arguments in the sixth-floor suite at the Mapes Hotel were loud and bitter. The relationship with the Kennedys, whatever it may or may not have been, enticed her. Pal Frank Sinatra owned the Cal-Neva Lodge at Crystal Bay Lake Tahoe. The lodge was an hour's drive from Reno, and Monroe sometimes snuck away to visit Sinatra there when the day's shooting was concluded. These were her happy times. Shortly before the film was finished, Sinatra threw a large party in the showroom and invited the entire cast and crew. Monroe, with husband Arthur Miller in tow, took him up on the offer.

Filming on *The Misfits* was completed, and Monroe, her marriage to Miller over, headed back to Los Angeles. Miller moved on and married photographer Inge Morath, who had also worked on *The Misfits*. Marilyn eagerly accepted her next role in *Something's Got to Give*—a comedy, just what she needed.

But she couldn't keep to a schedule, and her habitual tardiness irritated everyone on the set. She was getting older by Hollywood standards; younger stars waited in the wings. Studio bosses lost patience with her and terminated her services. It was a crushing blow, one she never recovered from.

Before the Mapes Hotel was imploded in 2000, some of those who worked security in the locked-up building claimed to encounter the ghostly Monroe from time to time. Wandering the hallways or laughing at some unknown joke in the old Skyroom, her specter is said to roam the spot where the hotel once stood. That is, when she's not haunting some other area of the world.

THROWING WEDDING RINGS

Early Reno movers and shakers wanted to keep Reno in the public eye. To that end, they devised one scheme after another to ensure the city space in the day's news. They had a little help from the politicians who shortened the

The Wedding Ring Bridge, circa 1905–1920. Note the early streetcar on the bridge. *Author's collection.*

divorce residency requirements and legalized gambling, but there needed to be more. Maybe they could build on the divorce industry.

He loves me, he loves me not—once a divorce was secured, and the divorcée stopped to kiss one of the courthouse pillars, you might have thought that good luck was ensured. But not so fast—Reno had another tradition. No one is sure where or when it began. Perhaps it was the description of a wedding ring being tossed into the Truckee that appears in Cornelius Vanderbilt Jr.'s 1929 novel *Reno*. Perhaps not, but one thing is certain: the tradition was meant to solve the vexing problem of what to do with the ring once the spouse was shed. If you've ever watched *The Misfits*, you've seen Marilyn Monroe and Thelma Ritter discussing the tossing of the ring on the Wedding Ring Bridge. That's it. When done with your spouse, toss your wedding ring into the Truckee River from the bridge. It was just one more way to ensure yourself a better matrimonial adventure the next time around.

Although some may argue and say it never happened, women have tossed their rings into the Truckee River. And now you know how the bridge became known as the "Wedding Ring Bridge" or the "Bridge of Sighs." And now you also know how many a teenage boy spent his Saturday afternoons back in the day—why, searching for gold at the bridge, of course. Whether or not the tossed ring increased one's odds in future marriages has yet to be determined.

WILHELMINA BECK'S SKULL

Love is blind. It can also be macabre, as this story of Mr. and Mrs. Beck demonstrates. Fire was always deadly in a time before high-tech firefighting equipment. One of the most devastating fires in Reno's early history was the conflagration that swept through the Commercial Row area on March 2, 1879. Fanned by fierce spring winds, the flames destroyed ten city blocks, while firemen courageously fought to contain the blaze. Total property damage was set at nearly $1 million. Among the smoldering ashes were the bodies of five people who had been trapped in wooden buildings that went up like matchsticks.

One of those who perished in the fire was Mrs. Wilhelmina Beck. It was her love of material things that cost her her life. She and her husband, John, operated a successful boardinghouse on Center Street in downtown Reno. When he realized the wind was whipping fire straight for their house, Mr. Beck raced home to warn his wife. However, she wasn't one to run out on the material things she'd worked so hard to achieve, and it was all in the basement. She waved her husband on and agreed to meet up with him later.

But the flames were swift. Once she got down into the basement, Mrs. Beck was trapped there and died, as the burning building crashed in upon her. When the embers cooled, the heartbroken Mr. Beck sifted through the rubble. What could possibly have meant so much to her that she would have died for, he wondered. Nothing seemed worth it. And then he happened upon something very valuable—to him, at least. This was a treasure that he would conceal and carry in his long coat for the rest of his days and nights.

And so it went. Whenever the thirsty (he was always thirsty, by most accounts) Mr. Beck met someone in the saloon and they happened to ask how he was doing, he had a stock response. "I'm fine," he would say. And throwing open his coat he would pull out the skull of his dearly departed missus and add, "And Mrs. Beck is doing fine as well."

Both Becks are buried in Reno's old Hillside Cemetery if you'd care to pay your respects. And Mrs. Beck's skull? That's the question, isn't it?

THE UNLUCKY MYRON LAKE AND THE LAKE MANSION

Regardless of whether it was the old iron bridge, the current Wedding Ring Bridge or the new proposed bridge, Reno's history begins at the Virginia Street Bridge, more or less.

The Truckee River flows under the bridge. Beginning its downward descent high in the Sierra, the Truckee, swollen with spring runoff from melting snow, rushes east past Verdi, along the railroad tracks and Interstate 80, through downtown and onward to Pyramid Lake, where it is swallowed up in the vast saltwater lake and forgotten.

The Truckee has played a part in Reno since its beginnings. During recent excavations for the new train trench, several artifacts were unearthed. The discovery of these implements indicates that early people lived along the banks of the Truckee hundreds of years before silver was discovered in Virginia City.

The Comstock's silver rush and ensuing rush to Washoe were the impetus for a businessman by the name of Fuller to build his toll bridge at the site of the present-day Riverside Artists Lofts. Cattlemen, sheepherders and anyone else wishing to cross from one side to the other either paid the toll or didn't cross.

This seemed like a profitable business to Myron Lake, who purchased the toll-crossing operation from Fuller, thus giving Reno its first name, Lake's Crossing. Eventually, city fathers would agree that it was a very good business—lucrative yet illegal (since it was a public thoroughfare that belonged to citizens anyway), and Lake was forced to give it up.

The road was a public thoroughfare; the toll bridge would be taken down. An iron bridge was erected over the Truckee. The railroad was coming through.

Bad luck for Myron, but trust me, it got worse. Myron Lake and his wife, Jane, were experiencing marital difficulties. Perhaps, he reasoned, a new house would put an end to the problems. But not just any house. The house he wanted to present to Jane was at the corner of California Avenue and Virginia Street. It was a mansion, and wouldn't she be pleased? Built in 1877, the home was one of the finest in Reno. It was occupied by its builder, W.J. Marsh. After spending only two years in the home, Marsh moved his family out and sold it to Myron Lake.

Jane Lake agreed with Myron that the mansion was lovely, but she steadfastly refused to move into it with him. He realized she was serious when she filed for divorce. Taking the hint, he moved from the home they shared. But fate, as it often is, was cruel. Myron Lake would never live in the mansion that would one day bear his name.

It wasn't until 1888, four years after Myron Lake's death, that Jane and her children finally moved into the elegant house at the corner of California Avenue and Virginia Street.

The Lake Mansion in its original location, circa 1930–40. A gas station was built here later. *Author's collection.*

We call the Lake Mansion "Reno's mobile mansion" for good reason. It has stood at three different locations since it was built in 1877. With the 1970s came sweeping changes for the Reno area. New freeways were being built, and the city's population was swelling. Within twenty years, new housing communities and shopping malls would be scattered from one end of the Truckee Meadows to the other.

The old would have to make room for the new, and although it had played a significant part in early Reno history, the Lake Mansion was scheduled for demolition. Progress dictated that "Reno's First Address" be razed or moved elsewhere. A nonprofit organization was formed, and on July 29, 1971, the mansion was painstakingly relocated three miles south to the corner of South Virginia Street and Kietzke Lane on the grounds of the Reno-Sparks Convention Center. And there it stood, somewhat incongruous at its new location. It was a symbol of an earlier time in Reno, and more importantly, it was a symbol that our city's history was precious and would be preserved.

It was while the mansion was at this location that the ghosts began to make themselves obvious. A friend who worked at the Lake Mansion at this time told me the following:

Lake Mansion is definitely haunted. I heard footsteps on the stairs, and when I commented about it, co-workers nodded and said, "Oh, you've heard the ghost."

I wanted to do a presentation in the mansion that would require me to move things around. The historical society gave their permission, provided I put everything back exactly as it had been. So I carefully numbered every item and noted its location so that there could be no mistake where everything belonged. Next morning, I walked into the mansion and found everything had been moved around again.

My friend's story about the ghostly activity at the Lake Mansion aroused my curiosity and that of fellow ghost-hunting friends. We asked for and received permission to conduct a daylight investigation of the Lake Mansion. We arrived early, parked on the grounds and entered the mansion, armed with our equipment. We agreed it was exquisite but small for a mansion. However, thinking of the time period in which the house was built, we reconsidered. Recorders were turned on, and cameras were at the ready. Did anyone sense Myron Lake's presence in this house? Surprisingly, or maybe not so, we did. If he truly loved the mansion and was not permitted to reside in it in life, he may have returned in death to haunt it.

EVP was recorded. We came away convinced the mansion might just be haunted, and maybe one of the spirits is that of Myron Lake himself. We did record the sound of a woman's soft laughter and of a man's voice plaintively calling, "Jane."

Was it Myron? We wanted to think it was, but more investigations were needed.

And then it was time for the mansion to move once again. The convention center needed more parking spaces, and Lake Mansion would need to find a new location or once more face demolition. Grant money and donations were raised, and early on the morning of July 11, 2004, the mansion was slowly moved three miles north to its present location at the corner of Court Street, Flint Street and Arlington Avenue. Ironically, this is only a few blocks from its original location at the corner of California Avenue and Virginia Street.

Did the ghosts move with the mansion? If you're asking if it is still haunted, the answer is yes. Psychics who have visited the mansion have picked up on the spirits that reside here. There are footsteps, disembodied laughter, cold spots and other subtle signs that ghosts are about. During the Reno Ghost Walk, someone occasionally catches a glimpse of what appears to be a ghost in the parlor. Skeptics have pointed out that moving shadows are cast not by ghosts but by cars driving down Arlington Avenue. Could be, but either way, the Lake Mansion is a delightful must-see part of Reno's historic past.

Chapter 5

LOCATION, LOCATION, LOCATION

THE HAUNTED POST OFFICE

Better late than never—this is especially true regarding preservation of our unique buildings in Reno. While we lost the Mapes and others, some are being restored and preserved. The historic main Post Office in downtown Reno was built in 1933, and like the Washoe County Courthouse across the street (cattycorner), it was designed by Frederic DeLongchamps. It has been on the National Register of Historic Places since 1990. Thankfully, it will not be demolished. The post office has been renovated on the inside and will house office and retail space. Its new name will be 50 North Virginia. Amid all the la-di-da boutiques and shops, there will also be at least one ghost in residence, or so the story goes.

No one wants their hard work to be vandalized, so the new owners hired a man to guard the building at night to prevent break-ins. He may not have been a believer in the supernatural the first night he reported to work, but after encountering a ghostly postman a few times, he might have begun to wonder. This was not a postman from recent times. The guard described the ghost as wearing a uniform similar to what postmen wore in the 1930s to '40s era. It was obvious the ghostly postman meant no harm. He went about his work, seemingly unaware that time had passed.

There are two theories we can look at here, and the first involves the restoration. Ghost researchers are well aware that remodeling and restoration are surefire ways to increase ghostly activity. The next theory involves place memory—not a ghost in the true sense but rather a scene that

Construction of the post office in 1933. *Author's collection.*

The old post office at 50 North Virginia Street. *Photo by Bill Oberding.*

has embedded itself at a certain location. Think of a movie that replays one scene continuously and you get the idea. Either way, there is something out of the ordinary in the old post office.

MAPES HOTEL SITE GHOSTS

The end came on Super Bowl Sunday, January 30, 2000, when the City of Reno demolished the Mapes Hotel amid a strong public outcry. Not many of Reno's historic buildings remained. It was a bitter day for many longtime Renoites, as the Mapes held fond memories for so many. Sororities held their soirées in the Skyroom. Dinners, dancing and big-name entertainers of the era appeared at the Mapes. People like Frank Sinatra, Liberace, Jimmy Durante and Sammy Davis Jr. were among the names the Mapes offered its patrons. Whenever a Renoite wanted to do it up big, he or she generally chose the swank Art Deco–style building at 10 North Virginia Street for the event. When Marilyn Monroe and Clark Gable came to Reno for filming of *The Misfits*, the press was invited to meet the stars at the Mapes' Skyroom. Where else would such an event be held in those days?

But then on December 17, 1982, exactly thirty-five years after it opened, the Mapes shocked the city and its employees by abruptly closing up. The closure couldn't have come at a worse time. Winter is traditionally a tough time to be out of work in Reno's gaming industry. Business was slow, and no

one was hiring. Christmas was eight days away. While former Mapes employees pounded the pavement, the fine old building was boarded up and slowly emptied of its treasures. It remained, for over a decade, an eyesore and a sad reminder of just how quickly time had passed the Mapes by.

When it was finally imploded in 2000, the Mapes left its ghosts in search of new quarters. One of those thought to haunt the Mapes was John Richard Tinnes, a twenty-eight-year-old man who was going through a divorce

The Mapes Hotel, Wedding Ring Bridge and Truckee River (shortly before it was imploded). *Photo by Bill Oberding.*

when he walked into the hotel on February 7, 1947. No one saw him as he made his way to the roof. An article in the *Reno Evening Gazette* on February 7, 1947, reported, "Man Plunges to Death from Building Top. Divorce Seeker's Act Said Suicide in Police Report. The body struck in the street at the southeast corner of the intersection, narrowly missing a pickup truck stopped at the red light there. Death was instantaneous, according to Coroner Harry Dunseath."

Tinnes may wander the Mapes site still. The other obvious spirit here is the ghost of Marilyn Monroe, or at least a blond woman who resembles her. Security guards, who worked in the building from the time it was closed until it was imploded, reported seeing this apparition throughout the building.

The Mapes Hotel. *Photo by Bill Oberding.*

But not to worry about any homeless ghosts—these specters seem to have adapted well to their new home: the skate park that has replaced the Mapes.

Ghosts of the Riverside Artist Lofts

The Riverside Hotel was built in 1927 by George Wingfield. Designed by Nevada architect Frederick de Longchamps, the building, with only six floors, was Reno's tallest and grandest. This was exactly what Wingfield wanted in order to take advantage of Reno's growing divorce trade.

Nevada's waiting period for a divorce was the shortest in the country, and Reno quickly became the Divorce Capital of the World. Divorce was big business. In addition to the services of an attorney, all those people coming to Reno needed a place to stay. Wingfield wanted his Riverside to attract the wealthier among them. The women, and occasionally men, with mucho money liked the Riverside's elegance and locations, and here they stayed, even if only long enough to obtain a divorce and move on.

Reno's divorce business fell in the 1940s, when Las Vegas got in on the action and other states relaxed their requirements. But the Riverside remained a favorite with tourists. A succession of owners and managers, including Jesse Beck and Pick Hobson, operated the Riverside Hotel after George Wingfield.

As the twentieth century came to a close, someone came up with a great idea. Rather than demolish the old Riverside Hotel, why not convert it to apartments for local artists? Since 2000, the thirty-five low-income units have been rented out to local artists—actors, dancers, painters, singers and writers—who want to practice their art in downtown Reno without the high-class rent and prohibitive HOA fees that come along with Reno's downtown condos. Since it is a fabulous location with affordable rent, tenants probably stay until they die or hit the lottery.

Riverside Artist Lofts. *Photo by Bill Oberding.*

The only caveat is that those who reside here do so with ghosts. Caveat? In some circles, ghosts would be considered a perk. According to a tenant who occasionally steps out onto the sidewalk with her little dog during the Reno Ghost Walk, the ghost of Marilyn Monroe walks the hallways of the artist lofts. Apparently Monroe has added a new location to the list of places she chooses to haunt.

"I know it's her because I've heard her high heels," the resident claims.

Surely some other ghost could be wearing high heels. I know of one female ghost here, but she was quite elderly, probably not given to wearing high heels. But then again, if it's true that ghosts can appear at any age they choose, the old woman may have come back as her more youthful self.

Did Marilyn Monroe ever stay at the Riverside Hotel? Even if she did not, the proximity from here to the Mapes site is only a few yards, not to mention the nearby Wedding Ring Bridge. And it well could be that Monroe has decided to come over and see how things are at a different location.

Other tenants have told of the sound of giggling, like that of a young girl. And let's not forget the artist Marianne, who appeared every morning at the Dreamers Café for her latte. In her youth, she was a beautiful artist's model, and yes, she probably wore high heels—but I've jumped ahead of myself. Marianne appears in the next story.

DREAMERS CAFÉ GHOST

Dreamers Café was located inside the section of the building that was once part of the Riverside Hotel's casino floor. The café served up sandwiches, delectable milkshakes, lattes, Danish and cheesecake. Shortly before the café closed, I stopped by to hear about its ghost and inadvertently put myself in the middle of the story.

After greeting me warmly, the manager, Julie‡, said, "Take a seat, and I'll be with you in a just a minute."

I looked around and chose a table by the window. This way I could people watch while I waited. When she was finished with her barista duties, Julie joined me at the table. "Funny you picked this table," she said. "The chair you're sitting in is where the ghost sits."

---

‡ Not her real name.

She sat down and explained that the ghost was Marianne, a former artist's model who lived in the Riverside Artist Lofts. She came in every day, and she always wanted her latte extra sweet with lots of vanilla. After Marianne died, Julie and her crew noticed the chairs at her table pulled out.

"We like everything a certain way," said Julie. "We see that the chairs are all pushed in under the tables at night. But in the morning the chairs at this table are always pulled out, like someone is sitting in them. She's a nice spirit. There is nothing negative about her."

I had to agree with her on that. I may have been sitting in her chair, but Marianne the ghost was being very polite about it.

Julie had another ghostly incident to share. "My barista station is off limits to customers. Sometimes a customer will walk through thinking it is the door to the bathroom. One night I thought someone had wandered in, so I was ready to point them in the right direction. As I looked up, I saw a woman's leg in black stocking and black pump with a little heel, like something from in the 1800s. A costume, I told myself. So I went back to tell her no one is allowed in here, but there was no one there."

Julie also told me about something weird that had happened at the nearby restaurant Wild River Grille. The restaurant was closed for the day. The bookkeeper was deep in her work when she noticed someone come into the room. Not wanting to be disturbed, she said, "I'll be with you in just a moment," and kept going over her figures. When she finished, she looked up and asked, "Yes, what is it?"

To her amazement, the man standing at her desk had vanished.

BRUKA THEATRE

In his poem "Haunted Houses," Henry Wadsworth Longfellow wrote, "All houses wherein men have lived and died are haunted houses." He was right. And taking this a step further, I believe it also stands to reason that theaters are haunted as well. Think of all the emotions, real and feigned, that are played out night after night in the theater. Think of the superstitions, the actors, the energy and the egos, and you get the idea here. Superstition is strong in theaters, and it demands that "Good luck" and "Macbeth" never be uttered at the theater. Hence actors tell one another to "break a leg" and talk about "the Scottish play."

The Bruka Theatre is a non-equity and not-for-profit theater company with over two decades in downtown Reno. Located at the corner of North

Virginia and First Streets, the Bruka is just down the block and across the street from the Pioneer Center for Performing Arts. Got your bearings? Good, now let's discuss ghosts.

After having attended plays at the Bruka, I was very excited to be conducting my Ghosthunting 101 class there. Participants would hear my lecture (lucky them) and afterward do some ghost investigating in the building. A little research told me that the Bruka was a haberdashery at one time. The building was very old, though the façade was new. The tale they tell at the Bruka is that of a ghostly woman who screams when she is alone in the building. How do we know this if she is alone? Must be like that tree in the forest. At any rate, she screams, and she would be the first person we would attempt to contact. "Why are you screaming?"

The night finally came. There were about twenty of us ready, with cameras, recorders, dowsing rods, K-2s and other ghost-hunting gadgets. The class would be conducted in the smaller and cozier sub-Bruka area. Lecture over, we began the investigation. Because there were so many of us, we broke into smaller groups to keep from tripping over one another. A woman was sensed in the dressing room—not the screamer, but an actress. She did not belong to the theater, but she had come by and decided to stay. Ghosts sometimes do this. They will pass through, and when they find a suitable location—voilà, a haunting.

In the seating area, some who were psychic picked up the presence of a woman and a man, neither of them happy. Down in the basement area, there were high readings on the K-2s and some negativity—enough so that there were a few people who could not stand to be in the area. We concluded that the Bruka is haunted. As for the screamer, she was a no show. But then again, she was not alone in the theater.

Reindeer Lodge

Nothing lasts forever. The Reindeer Lodge, a place near and dear to Renoites, is closed. The Reindeer Lodge—does the name evoke thoughts of colorful hand-knit sweaters, designer boots and après skiing cocktails by a roaring fire in some chichi roughhewn lodge? This was not that place. But Reindeer Lodge had its own charm, albeit different than that of other businesses along the Mount Rose Highway. The rustic lodge had been here on the road to Tahoe for over fifty years. There was an eclectic outdoor collection that some may call an eyesore (but isn't beauty in the eye of the beholder?) of old tractors, fire trucks and farming implements. You name it, and you just might find it here. You would also find ski mobile rentals in the winter (when we got snow) and horseback rides in the summer. Some who stayed here have told about an unearthly shriek that sometimes echoes through the pines.

Although they'd heard the shriek and the sound of ghostly footsteps, no one was sure just who or what it was. Perhaps the sound was merely an owl or a bear—or Bigfoot. But then again, it could be some ghost letting off a little good-natured steam.

Besides the shriek and the ghostly footsteps, the spirit seemed to take delight in pranks like toppling bottles and playing with the water faucet. No one was ever certain who he was in life, though there are plenty of rumors. One story is that he was killed in a fight over a prostitute at the lodge in the early 1950s. Another tale is that he was a former tenant who died there in the early 1970s and isn't about to let death evict him from his happy home. Bigfoot or a ghost, either way there was something up at Reindeer Lodge.

GHOST AT THE ANTIQUE MALL

Aside from a cemetery or museum, what could be more natural for a ghost to haunt than an antique store? Think of all those possessions that belonged to long-dead people. Some of them may not have been happy to part with their treasures—so unhappy, in fact, that they cling to them even after death. Think not? If locations can be haunted, why not material objects? I say they can and sometimes are. This has never stopped me from indulging myself with antique costume jewelry and vintage clothing. To find such treasures, one must haunt antique stores. So it was on a sunny afternoon that some friends and I stopped in at the Antiques and Treasures Antique Mall on Sierra Street downtown.

We found an array of interesting items. You name it, they have it. We circled the mall a couple times, our arms laden with goodies. But did we sense anything unusual here? There is always the possibility that a ghost is lurking among the racks of old forty-five records or those of the Coro rhinestone earrings. I opted for two wine goblets that were used to toss back red or white about the time Marilyn Monroe was being lauded at the Mapes Skyroom, adding them to my stash. And then we asked the man who rang me up, "Is this place haunted?"

"I've never seen anything," he answered. "But there's a ghost here, and I've heard him. This always happens when I am working downstairs, usually around six o'clock in the evening. I hear footsteps come through the front door and walk to the middle of the store and stop. The first few times I heard him, I ran upstairs thinking someone was in the store, but there wasn't."

"Why do you think it's a man?" I asked.

"Heavy footsteps and the way he walks. I also know that people are uncomfortable in one area downstairs where the clothes are," he said.

I'd been down there and felt nothing except the disappointment of finding a beautiful jacket that was two sizes too small for me. Hmmm. I guess you could call that uncomfortable.

The mall is one of my favorite places to shop for antiques in Reno. I've been back several times and even bought what I consider to be a haunted doll there. Is she or isn't she? Like beauty, "haunted" is in the eyes of the perceiver.

WELLS AVENUE HOUSE

It's an old brick house, probably built sometime in the 1930s or '40s, a time before Wells became such a heavily traveled avenue. "Charming" is how the rental agency described it to the young couple, and the house was that, with its covered front porch, sunny kitchen, bathroom tile work and bay windows. The backyard was made that much smaller by the tall trees and rose and lilac bushes. A long-ago owner probably planted the trees, roses and lilacs in anticipation of the day they would look as grand as they did on this late spring day. There were drawbacks; the traffic was heavy at times, and it was clear across town from their jobs. But the rent couldn't be beat. The couple was impressed and eagerly shelled out their deposit money, signed a six-month lease, went back to their cramped apartment and started packing. Two days later, they were living in their new house. And the haunting started.

At first, the noises were attributed to trucks and cars driving past. But as the rumbling continued late into the night when there was barely any traffic, they realized something was wrong. They checked the house from top to bottom to see where the strange sound was coming from. Nothing that could cause the noise was found. A call to the rental agency sent a handyman and an electrician to conduct their own search and evaluation. Their results were the same—nothing.

The couple might have been able to deal with the rumblings if what they called a "shadow man" hadn't started appearing in the kitchen. The somber, dark, shadowy figure of a man would appear either at the back kitchen door or in the small living room, and then he would be gone. Well, they didn't watch television for nothing. The couple knew this was a ghost, and now they just had to figure out the best way to send it on its way. They called in a local ghost-hunting group, which promptly decided that the house was built on an Indian burial ground. They would smudge it and bless it, and hopefully the ghost would skedaddle. But it didn't. A psychic came and told them to try talking with the spirit. This they did. But the spirit wasn't interested in a conversation, and the rumblings grew louder.

Slowly, the woman began to realize something else. Whenever the shadow man appeared, the aura of the room would change from happy to ominous, and the couple would argue. Over silly things and serious things, but argue they did, almost like the shadow man had willed it.

Their dream house had turned into a dark and foreboding nightmare, and they wanted out. But there was the six-month lease to consider. The rental agent didn't want to talk about ghosts or unexplained noises, and certainly there was no way they were getting out of the lease without paying. Then came the threat of attorneys and suits and all those things that can kiss away one's savings faster than you can say *Nolo Contendere*. In the end, the couple paid and moved on. The house is still there, and occasionally it comes up for rent.

CALIFORNIA AVENUE MANSION

Meanwhile, on another side of town, a world apart, sits this mansion on California Avenue. You'd better have old money and lots of it in your deep designer pockets to live here. She didn't, but she married it—like a fairy tale come true, complete with a palatial home to call one's own. It had an expansive lawn that went on and on, crystal chandeliers, gleaming hardwood floors and a staircase straight out of a Hollywood movie set. You get the idea.

She was always happy here. Even with the ghost. Or was she? She saw her one night right after dinner: a woman with gleaming honey-colored hair, wearing a red dress that resembled fashions of the 1930s or '40s. The woman came running down the staircase, smiling and expectant, and just before she got to the bottom stair, she vanished. This wasn't the only time the woman saw this apparition, and she tried talking to the ghost and ignoring it. Still, on certain evenings, the girl would come running down the stairs full of happy anticipation.

What had put the ghost here? Had her lover jilted her? Had she died in that beautiful red dress in some horrible way? No records of any such event ever taking place could be found. But there she was, the honey-haired woman, running down the stairs.

I was told this story by a friend of a friend of a friend several years ago. I don't know what the woman did about her ghost or if, in fact, she still lives there on California Avenue. But if you're asking me, I don't think she was dealing with a ghost but rather a residual haunting, or place memory; these are more common than people realize. This might explain why there was no acknowledgement on the ghost's part. Think of it this way—you can talk back to a movie if you want, but you won't be getting a response. This is like a scene from a movie playing over and over. Or possibly it's a time-space continuum, time warp or time overlap, all of which are way out of my field of expertise.

LEVY MANSION/HAUNTED BOOKSTORE

I'll start this one off by acknowledging that not everyone believes in ghosts, and that's okay. Not every bookstore is housed in a purported haunted house. But Sundance Books is. The Levy Mansion was built in 1906 by local merchant William Levy. But Levy's wife, or so the tale goes, unhappily moved in because her home was facing a blue-collar street. She wanted her front door to face the more aristocratic California Avenue. An unhappy wife equals a miserable man, so Levy called in workmen to fix the problem and make his and his wife's lives happy once again. The mansion was turned so that the front side door became the front door. I had my doubts about this story when I first heard it, but now I think it's true.

Because of its history and haunted reputation, I was involved in numerous ghost investigations inside the mansion. One fall night, a few of us were standing at a north window upstairs when we saw movement. Was it a ghost? We stepped back, but something was staring at us through the window. It had to be a ghost because no one was that tall. Stepping up to the windowpane, we saw a pair of eyes looking back at us. No, it wasn't a ghost—it was a raccoon. I used to take the Reno Ghost Walk by the Levy Mansion. At least once a week, someone would claim to see children on the staircase as we walked up to the front door.

We invariably told them that the place was closed and no one—especially a child—was inside. Most accepted our explanation, but one woman didn't. She stood there looking through the front door, giving us a blow-by-blow account of the children who were at play inside.

Several ghost investigations had taken place in the mansion, which has served as a beauty salon, tattoo parlor, office space and now Sundance Books. Now that the Levy Mansion houses a bookstore, I don't see the spirits ever leaving. Can you think of a better place to haunt? I can't.

HILLSIDE CEMETERY

In his fascinating *Spoon River Anthology*, Edgar Lee Masters wrote about the lives and loves and dreams of many individuals buried in the local cemetery. Early on, Masters tells his reader, "All are sleeping, sleeping, sleeping on the hill."

Over the years, some of those sleeping in Reno's cemeteries have not done so peacefully. They have been rudely relocated. While this might be unheard of in other parts of the country, it has been done here in Reno more than once. An area near Hug High School in the northeastern part of the city was once a cemetery. The dead don't pay taxes, and they don't vote, so when the land was needed by the living for homes, a school and a highway, the occupants were disinterred and moved west to Our Lady of Sorrows Cemetery.

Hillside Cemetery is Reno's oldest. The forty-acre parcel of land opened for residents in 1875. There are 1,434 people resting (or not) here. While many of Reno's early pioneers rest here now, Hillside Cemetery may one day face a similar fate to those in northeast Reno. Because of its proximity to the University of Nevada–Reno, some want to see the old cemetery cleared, the bodies disinterred and new university dorms built on the site. Thoughts of the movie *Poltergeist* come to mind here.

There have been many stories of frat house parties among the tombstones. Beer bottles and other litter were strewn about the cemetery and headstones destroyed. Sadly, the nearly forgotten cemetery has been the victim of this careless vandalism and misuse over the years. Time will tell whether it will be cleared and dorms erected.

Cemeteries may not be the most haunted of places, but the following illustrates that ghosts truly can be anywhere and everywhere. The person who shared this incident with me worked as a dealer at one of the downtown casinos in 1975. As long as weather permitted, he chose to walk to work rather than drive. On this particular afternoon, the temperature soared toward the one-hundred-degree mark as he headed toward his job. In a hurry to get to the air-conditioned comfort of the pit, he varied his route and took a shortcut through the Jewish section of the cemetery.

For some reason he has never been able explain, he felt compelled to glance over his shoulder. Standing a few feet to his left was a tall woman wearing a long black woolen dress, and a black hat and veil obscured her face. As he watched her, he wondered why anyone would come out on such a hot day as this in such heavy clothing.

He didn't know if he should speak to her or not, so he turned away for a brief moment to think about it. He decided he would speak. But when he turned back to comment on the weather, she had vanished. He looked around the headstones and down the paths, but she was nowhere in sight.

Although he walked through the cemetery many times since that afternoon, he never again saw the mysterious woman in heavy black garb. He does not believe in ghosts, but he is still not convinced that what he saw in the Hillside Cemetery that afternoon wasn't a ghost.

A couple was walking through the cemetery one evening when they happened to stop at a grave that appeared to be sunken. While they stood talking, the young woman felt a blast of cold air. She didn't say a word, but when they got back to their car, the man asked, "Didn't you feel that cold air at the broken grave? What do you suppose it was?"

How many people are killed at a cemetery? I'd bet there aren't very many, but Bill Blanchfield was.

It was a warm summer day on August 1, 1924, at the Knights of Pythias section of the Hillside Cemetery. Mourners were gathered for the funeral of Samuel Gerran, a dear friend of Bill Blanchfield. Reverend Brewster Adams was officiating. Circling overhead was Blanchfield, in his de Havilland biplane, waiting to pay a final tribute to his longtime friend. His plan was to pass over three times and to drop a wreath onto the flag-draped coffin on the final pass. As it came in for its second pass, the plane was so low to the ground that mourners could see Blanchfield in the open cockpit. In his hand was the wreath.

Then something went wrong. Just as the plane turned south for the third and final pass, a sudden gust of wind hurled it downward. Before Blanchfield could regain control, the plane nosedived into a tangle of telephone wires and slid into the side of a nearby house. Witnesses reported "a blood-curdling scream" at the instant of impact. The gas tank exploded, sending flames in all directions. The fires completely destroyed the house, but luckily its occupants had escaped safely.

Bill Blanchfield met death here at the Hillside Cemetery, and he may be the ghostly man some claim to have encountered here, but he is buried at Mountain View Cemetery in Reno. He is in good company at Mountain View; Reno mayor E.E. Roberts rests here, as does Senator Pat McCarran.

DONNER PARTY GHOSTS OF RATTLESNAKE MOUNTAIN

For two days in February 2005, the *Reno Gazette Journal* carried an unusual story. Several motorists had reported seeing a little girl crossing a busy section of McCarran Boulevard near Mira Loma Street in south Reno late at night.

This was the dead of winter. Temperatures were in the twenties, and the child, according to everyone who had seen her, was clad only in a nightgown. Reno police officers canvassed the area in search of the little girl. When they couldn't find her, they knocked on doors and attempted to discover who she was and what she was doing out alone on a cold, wintry night. They turned up nothing. No one had any answers, and so the mystery went down as unsolved.

It's interesting that this location is very near the area where the Donner Party camped during their sojourn here in the Truckee Meadows. A ghostly child has been seen more than once in the area of the memorial plaque that marks the site. Was the little girl an apparition or was she a living, breathing child who successfully sneaked out of her home not once but twice? I'm betting she was the latter.

The Donner Party arrived in the Truckee Meadows in what is present-day Reno in the late summer of 1843. Tired and weary after their long trek across the Forty-Mile Desert, they camped at a spot near the base of Rattlesnake Mountain. Water was plentiful, the weather was warm and inviting and they stayed longer than they should have. Those experienced with the vagaries of the Sierras cautioned the group's leaders to cross the mountains as soon as possible. Their warnings fell on deaf ears. The decision would cost them dearly.

Today, the area where the Donner Party camped is known as Donner Springs. Houses, condos and apartments cover most of it. Donner Park,

Above: Donner Park in Reno. *Photo by Bill Oberding*

Left: Monument to the Donner Party. *Photo by Bill Oberding*

The area at the base of Rattlesnake Mountain in Donner Park in Reno where a ghostly little girl was sighted. *Photo by Bill Oberding.*

a small neighborhood park, has been created near the spot where they camped. A monument here honors the ill-fated Donner Party.

I'm not quite sure whether the following has anything to do with the Donner Party. When I received a call from a woman who lived in one of the newer apartments in the Donner Springs area, I was intrigued. She couldn't understand why her ultra-modern apartment was being haunted by two children who, in her words, "looked like they were from an old television western."

This was the first time I'd heard such a story, but it wouldn't be the last. A man who was living in the Millcreek Townhomes in this area near Rattlesnake Mountain changed his mind about ghosts one night when he heard what he thought was an intruder. When he saw a shadow flit across the room, he jumped up, ready for action. It was an intruder all right—of the ghostly sort.

The Reno Haunted Bus Tour was stopped at the plaque commemorating those who'd come west. It was a dark October night, and a chill was in the air. We got out with flashlights in hand, but no one wanted to be off the bus for long. We gathered around the monument, reading its inscription. Our driver, who had stayed aboard, suddenly came flying off the bus. "Did you see that?" he asked.

No one had. "What was it?" I asked.

"A little girl—I saw her walk across over there," he pointed toward Rattlesnake Mountain. "She was glowing all white. Didn't anyone see her?"

We pointed our cameras in the direction and tried to take some shots. But none of us was able to get any good photos. Weeks later, another person on the tour caught a glimpse of the little girl in the same area. Was she a member of the Donner Party or someone entirely different? As we contemplated the question, I remembered that a member of the Donner Party had died in this vicinity. However, no children in the party died here. The ghostly little girl may have returned here because this was the last place on earth where she'd spent any happy, carefree moments.

As the bus pulled out onto the busy McCarran Boulevard, I told myself that this probably wasn't the last encounter with the Donner ghosts.

CHINA HOUSE GHOSTS

Today the only thing on this busy corner of South Virginia Street and Mall Way is the Meadow Wood Mall sign. This is a prime area of the city, so that could change at any time. Twenty years ago, the China House Restaurant stood here in this spot, just one of a long succession of restaurants that came and went. Long before the restaurants, an out-of-town gambling club called the West Indies occupied this space.

A mysterious death that began at the West Indies in 1948 may account for the ghost of the China House. This ghost was a nuisance. Taking great pleasure in moving kitchen utensils around, the ghost also lit a candle and left it in the front of the restaurant one night. There was a rumor that someone was lynched from a nearby tree long ago, but there is no record of it, so the story stays in the rumor column for now. But the ghost of the China House was real and just nerve-wracking enough to make the owners of the restaurant tell their story to the local news media. The ghost would move things around and at one point even left candles burning in the middle of the floor.

Is it possible that a man who died miles away, in the current location of the Sierra Summit Mall, had something to do with this haunting? Let's look at his story.

In the fall of 1948, Mrs. John Steinbeck (Gwyn Conger) came to Reno to serve the required six-week residency, divorce her husband and move on. Unlike some of the other women who came to town seeking their freedom, money was not a problem for Gwyn Steinbeck. She chose to establish residence at the popular Silver Saddle Ranch located on Holcomb Lane south of town. As it happened, an acquaintance, Leonard Wolff, a member of a wealthy Denver family, was also in town to shed a spouse. Reno was a small town in the 1940s, and eventually their paths crossed.

On the last night of Wolff's life, he and Mrs. Steinbeck met his parents at the Mapes Hotel for dinner in the Skyroom. After dinner and cocktails, the foursome parted company. Wolff and Steinbeck stayed and gambled a while at the Mapes and then headed out to the West Indies Club on South Virginia Street for a nightcap and more gambling. The soon-to-be-divorced Mrs. Steinbeck played a dollar slot machine while Wolff tried his luck at the blackjack tables. Hours passed. He increased his wagers from $25 a hand to $100. His losses were mounting, and the losing streak continued. When she ran out of silver dollars, Steinbeck told him goodnight, went out to the car and fell asleep. Wolff continued to play and to lose. It would be daylight before he stopped playing. In the six hours he'd played cards at the West Indies, Wolff had lost $86,000. To cover his losses, he wrote a check to the club's owner, Newell Benningfield, and stepped outside.

Steinbeck was sound asleep in his car. Without waking her, he started the car and drove toward the Silver Saddle Ranch. There, he woke her and promised to see her later in the day. When the bank opened that morning, Benningfield attempted to cash Wolff's check. A sharp-eyed teller checked the signature and refused to honor it. Apparently, the signer had neglected to add his middle initial when signing, and therefore it was not his legal signature.

A few hours later, Wolff's wrecked car was found just off the Mount Rose Highway (where the Sierra Summit Mall is today). His lifeless body was found slumped in the driver's seat with a bullet wound to the head. Beside him was a gun. Later, witnesses would say they saw his car speed up the curve and run off the highway. When they stopped to offer him assistance, he waved them on. Had Leonard Wolff met death by his own hand in the sagebrush-strewn area south of town, or was it something more sinister?

A few months later, Newell Benningfield attempted to collect his gambling debt from Leonard Wolff's estate by suing in the amount of $86,000. The judge ruled in favor of the late Wolff's estate. The debt could not be collected. Undeterred, Benningfield took his case to the Nevada Supreme Court. Unfortunately for him, the court upheld the previous judge's decision. No dice. The debt could not be collected. And that was the end of that. Or was it? Was Leonard Wolff murdered? If so, did he return, seeking justice at the spot where the old West Indies once stood?

HAUNTED KITCHENETTE

When it was built decades ago, the motel on South Virginia Street was considered to be on the outskirts of town. Since then, the city has grown, and today the motel is surrounded by strip malls, car lots and fast-food restaurants. Its tenants are no longer travelers stopping by for the night; they live here as permanent residents.

The following was told to me by a couple who, like so many others in the early 1970s, came to Reno with more dreams than money.

After spending the day searching for affordable housing, they considered themselves lucky to have stumbled on the reasonably priced kitchenette on the edge of town. It was a small knotty pine unit, clean except for the odor of garlic permeating it. But the main appeal was the fact that their two young sons and their Great Dane were more than welcome.

They moved in, and all went well for nearly a week. Then the woman remembers waking to the sound of the dog snarling in a low protective growl. She sat up and looked around the room. Everyone was sleeping soundly, the door was bolted and she was so tired that she drifted back to sleep. A few nights later, she was startled by the sound of a child's laughter. One of the boys must be laughing in his sleep, she told herself. But there was no shaking the feeling of uneasiness that surrounded her now.

She told me:

> The first time I saw the ghost, the boys and I were putting a jigsaw puzzle together. I happened to look up and there was this little girl staring down at me.
>
> I gasped so loud that my husband asked what was wrong. I couldn't do anything but point at the ghost, but he looked right at it and didn't even see it.
>
> My youngest son told me that it was only Noreen and she'd lived here a long time ago. I noticed that the little girl's ghost smiled shyly at the mention of her name, then slowly dissolved.
>
> The next morning, I went to the manager's office and told him about the ghost.
>
> "Yep," he said. "Some folks seem to think that unit is haunted. 'Course, I don't believe in that nonsense myself. Did you see her?"
>
> I knew darn well that he knew more about the ghost than he was telling me because I'd never mentioned that it was a little girl.
>
> "Sad thing. They say she's the ghost of a little girl that got herself killed 'round here years back. 'Course I—"

"We'll be moving," I blurted out before he could finish. I ran back to the apartment and started to pack. There was just no way I was going to live with a ghost, friendly or not.

GALAXY CRASH

On the night of January 21, 1985, the unthinkable happened in Reno. Galaxy Airlines Flight 203 with seventy-one people onboard crashed onto South Virginia Street. A seventeen-year-old boy was the only survivor. Today it is a busy area of town with strip malls, motels and restaurants.

Many of the people who work at these places may not even know or remember about the Galaxy crash, and yet some claim to have seen the occasional shadowy figures or heard the disembodied voices. A man driving down the section of South Virginia Street just before dawn was alarmed to see two people dart out in front of his car. He threw on the brakes and readied for impact. There was none. He pulled to the side of the street and got out to see what had happened to them. Where had they gone, he wondered. He walked across the street and back, then up and down the block. There was no one on the street but him.

I was told by someone who claimed to have worked on the crash clean-up that he saw sights and sounds he would never be able to explain, much less talk about. When pressed for details, he said, "Working on that changed my whole perspective of what I believe about life and death."

And he would say no more.

RENO-SPARKS CONVENTION CENTER

When it was built in 1964, the Reno Convention Center was way out on the outskirts of town. It was called the Centennial Coliseum in commemoration of Nevada's centennial birthday that year. Since then, Reno has grown, and what was once the outskirts is now a busy, heavily traveled area of town. In order to keep up with the growth, the building has been enlarged and remodeled numerous times since 1964.

For many years, some employees claimed that the rooms in the B20 area were haunted by the ghost of a man who fell to his death during completion of the building. The ghost was known as Oscar. Most didn't mind a ghostly co-worker, but some absolutely refused to work alone in the area where the ghost was said to hang out.

"Just because you can't see him doesn't mean he isn't there," a former employee said of the ghost.

The ghostly Oscar was friendly, but he wasn't above a joke. Besides being blamed for an occasional icy draft that swept through the building, he was known to pull the plug on speakers' microphones during important business meetings, misplace workers' tools and cause the lights to flicker on and off.

"He patted me on the shoulder one night, and that was enough to make a believer out of me," a former employee said.

Oscar appeared before at least one employee in a rather strange way. That employee recounted: "One night I was working with a new man, and we kept seeing weird lights coming from the Virginia Street side of the building. We thought it was probably just car lights, but it was really late at night and we weren't sure. All of a sudden, we heard this *clip-clop, clip-clop* like noise and looked up to see legs—nothing but legs—walking down the corridor toward us. It must have scared [the new man] something fierce because he quit that very night. I don't understand because we'd already told him about Oscar."

Does Oscar still haunt the Reno-Sparks Convention Center? I decided to ask. Some former employees are convinced that he will be there forever. However, I was invited to give a presentation on Reno's ghosts at the Reno Comic Con recently, and in between gawking at the celebrities, I took the opportunity to explore the building. It was not an easy undertaking, considering all the people who came out for the comic convention, but I persisted. Three employees were asked about Oscar the ghost. Every one of them looked at me as if I had just lost my mind. They had never heard of Oscar or a ghost. Okay, it is definitely not a scientific poll, but there you have it. Perhaps Oscar has moved on to a new job elsewhere.

UNIVERSITY OF NEVADA–RENO

The University of Nevada was founded in Elko (about three hundred miles east of Reno) in 1874. The only problem was that most of the state's students lived in the Reno area. Leave it to the politicians to fix everything—almost everything, anyway. So in 1885, the Nevada legislature approved the relocation of the university from Elko to Reno. Here it became known as the University of Nevada–Reno (UNR).

The National Judicial College is located on the campus, as is the Nevada Historical Society and the Fleischmann Planetarium. The school's Mathewson-IGT Knowledge Center is a state-of-the-art all-media library. The school's basketball, football and baseball teams are the Wolf Pack.

The rivalry between UNR and the University of Nevada–Las Vegas (UNLV) is well known. The Fremont Cannon, a replica of the howitzer used by explorer John Fremont, is not only the heaviest but also the most expensive trophy in college football. Since 1970, the tradition is that the cannon travels back and forth between UNR and UNLV depending on which team wins that year's football game. When UNR wins, the cannon's carriage is painted blue; as the victor, UNLV paints it red. At this writing, the cannon carriage is blue.

UNR is a great school of which Reno is very proud, and like many other universities, there are some ghosts said to roam about the campus.

Built in 1885, Morrill Hall was the first (and thus, the oldest) building to be erected on the UNR campus. Located on the south end of the quad, Morrill

A front view of Morrill Hall. *Photo by Bill Oberding.*

A rear view of Morrill Hall from the Quad. *Photo by Bill Oberding.*

Lincoln Hall. *Photo by Bill Oberding.*

Hall shares a distinction with the Goldfield Hotel. Noted Reno architect M.J. Curtis was involved with the design of both buildings. And like that old hotel in Goldfield, Morrill Hall has its ghosts, albeit not as active or famous. Chilly unexplained breezes, ear-piercing screams that shatter the silence and a ghostly woman who peers from one of the upstairs windows are the activity usually reported here. No surprises here—this is an old building that has witnessed a lot. Before it had reached the century mark, Morrill Hall was placed on the National Register of Historic Places in 1974.

Next up in the oldest buildings on campus category are Lincoln Hall and Manzanita Hall. It figures that there are some stories about the hauntings of these buildings. There was some recent talk of tearing down Lincoln Hall, but good sense and preservationists persevered, and so it stands.

The specter residing at Lincoln Hall is thought to be that of James Champagne, a twenty-year-old student who died here in the winter of 1906. There are two very different versions of how James Champagne lost his life. One story has him committing suicide.

The ground was nearly frozen solid, the walkways were sheets of ice and icicles hung on tree branches that drooped with the very weight of them. While other students looked forward to the semester's end with its gaiety and laughter, Champagne was faced with a private dilemma. He chose to resolve it by shooting himself in Lincoln Hall.

As is said about suicide, it was a permanent solution to a temporary problem, and unfortunately, he has regretted that dreadful decision ever since—so much so that he refuses to leave the dormitory, semester's end or not. Strange noises are still heard in the dorm, and the ghost himself has been seen in the basement and other areas of the hall.

The other version of James Champagne's death has him absently cleaning his gun when it accidentally discharged, sending a bullet hurling into his chest. Fatally wounded, he staggered into the lobby begging for help. There he died.

But there is a third more sinister possibility. James Champagne did die in Lincoln Hall; we know this. He died of a gunshot wound, but what if he was murdered? What if Champagne had an enemy who shot him, for whatever reason, and then made the death look like an accident or a suicide? According to the February 13, 1906 issue of the *Reno Evening Gazette*, at inquest, the coroner's jury found the death accidental. One witness said that he had been in the reading room when Champagne came into the room. In his hand was a letter that he crumpled up and threw into the fireplace. "Look out!" the witness said he had told Champagne. "There might be a check in that letter."

"No, there's no check in that letter and there never was," Champagne had responded. He then left the room, and within minutes, the sound of a gunshot filled the hall. While Dr. Hood testified to caring for the deceased, he didn't mention hearing Champagne say anything. Richard Brown, however, did. He said that when he asked Champagne how it he happened, Champagne responded, "I was monkeying with the gun when it went off. It was accidental, Prof."

The article concluded, "Will Champagne, a brother of the deceased, testified that he received a letter from his brother and that in it his brother did not mention anything that would indicate that he intended to take his own life."

Most likely his death was a terrible accident, but given the forensics of 1906, we will never know for sure. James Champagne is buried in the Hansen plot at the Genoa Cemetery in Genoa, Nevada.

There are those who will say that there is no ghost in Lincoln Hall. To which I would answer, prove it! If ghost investigators are required to prove the existence of things that go bump in the night, surely nonbelievers must adhere to the same standards. Meanwhile, the sobbing and strange noises continue in Lincoln Hall.

Moving on to Manzanita Hall, we hear of the eerie sounds of a baby crying late into the night. No babies here, but the old tale is that of a young woman burying her newborn in the basement during construction of the building. Another story has the crying being that of a young woman who killed herself on the site when her true love jilted her for another.

Why on earth would Nye Hall be haunted? It's a good question, and I have an answer. The dormitory was built in the early 1960s on land that was once a cemetery. In order to make room for the new building, several bodies had to be disinterred and reburied elsewhere. It's not the first time this has happened, and it won't be the last. This is Nevada, and this is how we do things. However, you start messing around with someone's final resting place, and there's bound to be some repercussions. Although there have been no ghostly sightings in Nye Hall, there are those cold spots, the feeling of being watched and things that get misplaced. This could make for a new twist on the old "the dog ate my homework" excuse: "The ghost wiped my laptop clean. Yes, the laptop that all my notes and assignments were on." It works for me.

Several years ago, I was working with the Ghost Conference of Truckee Community College. As part of the event, we were permitted to investigate some of UNR's locations. Frandsen Humanities Building was one of these.

Statue of John Mackay, created in 1908 by sculptor Gutzon Borglum, who also sculpted the presidential busts of Mount Rushmore. *Photo by Bill Oberding.*

Located on one of the most picturesque spots on campus, near Manzanita Lake, Frandsen Humanities Building was constructed between 1917 and 1918. Employees told of doors that open and close of their own volition, whispered disembodied conversations and of "just knowing it's haunted." Unlike some of the other buildings, there is no backstory here that can be attributed as the cause of ghostly activity. This doesn't mean that Frandsen Humanities Building is not haunted. Those who've been in the building after dark insist that it is.

The Mackay School of Mines building was designed by noted architect Stanford White. Unfortunately, White didn't live to see his creation come to fruition. He was shot and killed by the husband of his lover, Evelyn Nesbitt Thaw, in what resulted in a scandal and the trial of the century. Reno architect Frederick De Longchamps did the 1926–29 remodel of the building.

Comstock silver baron John Mackay is connected to the Mackay School of Mines building and the Keck Museum located in the building. The connection is a large endowment the Mackay family bestowed on the university in honor of family patriarch John Mackay. But there is another connection here as well, and that is the large painting of Mackay's daughter-

A painting of Katherine Duer Mackay. *Photo by Bill Oberding.*

in-law Katherine Duer Mackay, the first wife of son Clarence. In it, Katherine poses holding a crystal ball, and in the forefront of the painting, a spirit rattle is depicted. During the 1988–92 renovation of the building, the great-grandson of Katherine Mackay discovered the painting in the basement. To his amazement, it was floating in the air. Today, the mysterious painting is

A painting of Dr. E. Richard Larson that hangs in conference room 302. *Photo by Bill Oberding.*

located in conference room 302 in the DeLaMare Library in the School of Mines building. Talk is that the ghostly Katherine is attached to the painting. Former employees who have been alone in the room with the painting say it holds a powerful energy that gives off a strong sense of eeriness. Everyone knows better than to try and move the painting. It has fallen from the wall whenever attempts have been made to hang it elsewhere.

When I visited conference room 302 recently, it had a calm and peaceful feel to it. It's a room I could get comfortable in, maybe read a good book or just relax and contemplate the stories surrounding it. One of those is the flickering lights. Whenever this happens, Katherine gets the blame, just as she does when some of the building's clocks stop for no earthly reason. But don't be so fast to blame the ghostly Katherine, say others who've worked here. Many believe it is the most haunted building on campus. Some employees say that the clocks in a certain room stop at the same time that geology professor Dr. E. Richard Larson died in 1979 here in conference room 302, which was his office in that year.

The stopping of a clock at the moment of someone's death is not as rare as it might seem. There's the tale that says all the clocks in his home and

The desk of Dr. E. Richard Larson in conference room 302. *Photo by Bill Oberding.*

workshop stopped running when Thomas Edison died on October 18, 1931. In the 1876 song "My Grandfather's Clock" by Henry Clay Work, there is a verse that goes "But it stopped short—never to go again—when the old man died."

Aside from a feeling of being haunted, other strange occurrences within the Mackay School of Mines building are the elevator that moves by itself and levitating items.

Founded in 1908, the Keck Museum is the oldest brick-and-mortar museum in the state of Nevada. Over 100,000 objects are housed in the museum. Among these items is a shrunken head from Ecuador. That's creepy, yes. But if you stop and think that most of the objects here were bequeathed by those who loved the items, you get an idea of how it's possible that the place could be haunted.

Reno Little Theatre

The Reno Little Theatre has been around since 1935. Originally located downtown at the corner of Sierra and Seventh Streets, the theater was razed in 1991 to make room for a casino parking lot. From there, the theater moved to its temporary location at the Reno Elks Lodge on Kumley Lane. In 2012, the theater moved into its new million-dollar facility on East Pueblo Street.

You just can't help but wonder how many ghosts the theater might have picked up in all this time. Ghosts, we know, have a special fondness for the stage. Perhaps it's the excitement, the emotions or the actors and actresses themselves that attract these spirits. Or maybe it's the thrill of curtain time and of taking an encore or two. Alas, it may be nothing more than ego. Whatever the reason, it is a difficult task to find a theater without at least one ghost in residence—just try.

Years ago, while at its downtown location, the Reno Little Theatre had a ghost affectionately known as George, a friendly phantom of whom staffers were quite fond. Even though he liked to misplace tools and other items, he would gladly return them when asked to do so. Some said they would occasionally catch a glimpse of the ghost out of the corner of their eyes, and others said they heard him walking across the empty stage from time to time. Has George moved to the new location, or has he moved on to tread the boards in another realm entirely?

THIRD STREET BAR

I was introduced to the Third Street Bar by my friend Debbie Bender, who owns the Bats in the Belfry Ghost Tour in Virginia City. She was right—the small neighborhood bar is a fun locals' hangout, reminiscent of something you might find in Bay Area neighborhoods. Built in 1920, the bar is a block west of the Eldorado parking garage downtown. It has gone through many owners, many uses and changes and names. Among its uses was as a real estate office and an awnings store, and according to some, the building was used as a slaughterhouse long ago. As creepy as that might sound, it is not the reason for the ghosts.

This, they say, happened when the bar was called Molly Malone's. It's a lurid story of a woman getting into a fight and being stabbed to death with a broken pool cue. There is another story of a heated argument that was taken out onto the sidewalk. Two people died as a result of the fight. All this happened in the bar and on the sidewalk, which is on the ground floor. This was one of Reno's roughest bars back in the day. If you were looking for trouble or a good fight, this is where you came. However, the paranormal activity here is said to be in the basement, where the slaughterhouse pit, in which the blood was drained, is still intact. Debbie and I did our own mini investigation of the bar. Then we hosted a meet and greet in which we invited a local ghost-hunting team to investigate the basement.

Photos were taken, and EVP sessions took place. Although minimal activity was collected, the belief was that this is indeed a haunted location. It was Wednesday night, and that is comedy night at the Third Street Bar. Up the stairs we went, ready for a good laugh and hoping that the ghosts here have senses of humor.

ROCK CITY POSTERS

Rock City Posters was located in the Midtown area of Reno. A hip, young, up-and-coming neighborhood of healthy natural food restaurants, wine and cheese stores, antique stores, used furniture shops, hardware store, tattoo parlors, vintage clothing—see where I'm going with this? It's an eclectic neighborhood, revitalized from the tired and broken-down place it once was to something vibrant. Rock City Posters was the perfect fit. Owner Scotty Roller is a musician and an artist who creates posters as Scotty Roller

Designs. The store was a gallery of gig posters old and new. Scotty offered some really cool stuff here—some expensive, some not so much. Anybody here a Billy Idol fan? Just asking. Whatever your musical tastes, there was a poster—and a ghost.

So how does one explain to a ghost that this is a different time, a different venue and a different neighborhood? Don't waste your time trying. If the ghosts aren't bothering you, then live with them. And that's what the people at Rock City Posters were doing, living with the ghost of Stanley. When I spoke with manager Nicky Clark, she told me that she's seen Stanley out of the corner of her eye many times. So who is Stanley and why was he haunting Rock City Posters? Nicky had an answer. Long before this area became known as Midtown, this was Reno's first gay bar, and Stanley was its bartender for years and years.

Time moved on, the bar closed and Stanley died. Apparently he hasn't gotten the memo. He's still hanging around, still building drinks, neat and muddled. Rock City Posters has closed the Midtown store. Stanley, no doubt, awaits new tenants.

ROBB CANYON

When someone comes to a ghost research investigator with questions about a haunting, it is not the task of the researcher to tell that person whether he or she has truly experienced ghost activity. Who knows better about what one is feeling than oneself? That said, I do believe that stories should be researched to see if there are historical aspects that offer confirmation. I realize this isn't always possible, but it should be at least attempted. This is one reason why I have doubts concerning some of the stories of the Robb Canyon haunting.

I did not want to include it here, but after some consideration, I realized that I couldn't write a book about Reno's ghosts, in good conscience, without including Robb Canyon, which is said to be one of the actively haunted areas of the western United States. Robb Canyon is in northwest Reno, part of Rainbow Ridge Park. Any ghost hunter worth his or her salt has gone out there to investigate at least once. It's a beautiful, serene area by day. However, it is supposed to become negative, foreboding and downright frightening after dark. Some brave souls who've trekked out there to see for themselves have come back with stories of being attacked by phantoms, experiencing feelings of apprehension and hearing strange noises.

But why is the canyon haunted? Trust me, there's always a story that explains a haunting. This one has a hiker discovering the remains of four murder victims buried in shallow graves out in Robb Canyon circa 1970. Back in the '70s, before urban sprawl hit fever pitch, this was a desolate area. It would have seemed like the perfect spot to hide a body or two or more. Since I didn't recall such a discovery ever happening (and this would have been big news in circa 1970 Reno), I checked the Washoe County Sheriff Department's website of unsolved murder cases. Sadly, there are a lot of them, but none of them match the story of the four murder victims out in Robb Canyon. The nearest unsolved crime to this area involved a woman's body being found at the Derby Dam exit near Verdi, a few miles away.

With apologies to Mark Twain, who said, "Never let the truth get in the way of a good story," I looked at the next possibility, which is so implausible that you wonder who would believe it. According to some websites, it was decided that the discovery of the four murder victims' remains would be kept secret from the public. Okay, but then why, and how, do we know about it today?

There is yet a third possibility, and that is that the murderer was apprehended, stood trial and faced justice. Imagine what a big story that would have been. It didn't happen. I think the story of the four victims' remains is nothing more than the stuff of urban legend. And since the ghosts out here are supposed to be emanating from those of the angry four whose deaths were never avenged, I remain unconvinced about this particular haunting, or at least its root cause.

I'm not saying that Robb Canyon isn't haunted. It may well be. Historians say this was an area in which the local Native Americans tribes, the Paiutes and the Washoe, lived. While I don't necessarily ascribe to the belief that an Indian burial ground is always actively haunted, this may account for some of the activity in Robb Canyon, at least.

CHISM HOUSE

Longtime Renoites can tell you that Chism Dairy and Chism Ice Cream were well-known names in the area until the 1960s. The two companies were created by John H. Chism and Edward Warren Chism, sons of Gardner Chism, who built the Chism House on West Second Street in the late 1880s. The house was extensively remodeled and landscaped several years later by John H. and his wife. Today, it is a favorite Reno wedding venue with area brides who like its lush grounds that offer a romantic and picturesque setting for that special day.

Some of those who've lived here at the Chism House say it is also a haunted house. In October 2010, the Nevada Paranormal and Ghost Series, presented by Truckee Meadows Community College, was permitted a rare ghost investigation of the stately old house. It was a small group, and we fanned out through the house. Psychics picked up a woman in the front room. They thought that she didn't necessarily live here but had chosen to drop in and see the house. This is an old section of town, near the Truckee River. It's not surprising that a ghost might drop in for a time.

Upstairs, a woman and a little boy were sensed. The child, they said, was not happy here; possibly he was ill or homesick. Equipment being used this night included dowsing rods, cameras, recorders and spirit boxes. An investigator saw something out of the corner of her eye and quickly turned her dowsing rods in the direction. "Did you ever live in this house?" she asked. "Please cross for no and uncross for yes."

The rods crossed, meaning no, the spirit had not lived here. She walked toward the kitchen and the dining room, where we had been told some activity took place. "Do you like us doing this investigation?"

The rods uncrossed, so whoever this spirit was, he or she was not opposed to ghost hunters. This is always good to know.

A hateful ghost can, and often does, cause any number of problems. Common problems in ghost investigating, like batteries being drained, are often caused by a ghost, but this is inadvertent. "Ghosts suck the energy out of batteries" is a well-known mantra among ghost hunters. Our group left the woman to communicate with the friendly spirit and went upstairs. For some, this was not as light and friendly as the downstairs area of the house. We asked the spirit box about this. "Is someone unhappy up here?"

"You know," was the reply.

But we didn't, and we said so. The spirit box responded, "Go now."

It was not a threat but a suggestion, and so back downstairs we went.

BOWERS MANSION

Bowers Mansion is not precisely in Reno city limits. Located on Highway 395 in Washoe Valley between Reno and Carson City, it's close enough to count as Reno's own. The mansion is open for tours during the summer and early

Bowers Mansion. *Photo by Bill Oberding.*

fall. Occasionally, a visitor might catch a glimpse of the ghostly Eilley Orrum Bowers as she glides through the mansion. Her beautiful home was taken from her in life, through foreclosure. In death, no one can evict her.

Eilley isn't the only ghost on the premises. Her daughter Persia and the apparition of a child, who drowned in one of the ponds long ago, also haunt the mansion and the grounds surrounding it. Sightings of a glowing green figure moving across the grounds were often reported when old Highway 395 passed closer to the mansion than it presently does. But the ghost sightings are nothing new. Stories about the mansion being haunted date back to the late 1800s, when area teenagers claimed they had encountered the mansion's ghosts.

Eilley left her native Scotland and arrived in the United States as the bride of a much older church deacon in the early 1800s. The marriage failed when her husband sought another wife. The idea of polygamy did not appeal to Eilley, who asked for and was granted a divorce. She remarried and accompanied her second husband, Mr. Cowen, a devout Mormon, to the Washoe Valley area. To help supplement their income, Eilley did laundry for some of the single men in the area. Unfortunately, her second marriage fared no better than the first.

When Brigham Young called for the Mormon settlers to return to Salt Lake, Mr. Cowen was only too happy to heed the call. Eilley was not. She liked the Washoe Valley and steadfastly refused to accompany her husband home.

A self-reliant woman, Eilley could not be dissuaded once her mind was made up. In the end, Mr. Cowen packed up and left her alone in Washoe Valley. A lesser woman may have been frightened at the prospect of having to fend for herself, but not Eilley. She relied on what she saw in her crystal ball, and she'd seen some grand times coming her way, including a handsome suitor.

Eilley moved up to Gold Hill, where the action was, and opened a small boardinghouse. Along came Lemuel "Sandy" Bowers, a handsome man in search of silver. He was just another miner rooming at Eilley's until he found himself down on his luck. When his money ran out, Sandy offered Eilley part ownership of a new claim he was working in lieu of room and board payment.

Here was opportunity, and Eilley grabbed it. The decision proved lucky for both of them. Romance blossomed, and within months, Sandy took Eilley as his bride. The Bowers were riding a winning streak. Their mine turned out to be one of the richest on the Comstock Lode.

They were wealthy beyond their wildest dreams, just as Eilley had seen in her crystal ball. But neither one of them was wise financially. "We got money to throw at the birds," Sandy boasted to friends. And throw they did. Sparing no expense, the Bowers built their large mansion in Washoe Valley, a short distance from the spot where Eilley had once scrubbed clothes for a living. The mansion was built of the best and costliest materials, and the door knobs and window fittings were all said to be made of silver.

While work was being completed on their mansion, the Bowers set off on a tour of Europe, where they purchased some of the finest furnishings that money could buy. Now that she was wealthy, Eilley decided that she would take tea with Queen Victoria while in England. In eager anticipation, she had a fabulous afternoon gown created especially for the occasion. One story goes that Her Majesty was not impressed with Eilley. Nouveau riche American miners were bad enough, but a twice-divorced woman was someone Victoria would not entertain. Another story says that Queen Victoria was in mourning for her beloved Albert and was not receiving any visitors at the palace. This is probably closer to the truth. Regardless, Eilley took the snub in stride and continued on with her buying and her sightseeing.

The Bowers happily returned to their mansion and their lavish lifestyle, but tragedy was set to strike. While on a short business trip to Virginia City, Sandy contracted pneumonia and died, leaving Eilley heartbroken and penniless.

No sooner was Sandy interred in back of the mansion than the creditors began clamoring for payment. Apparently, Sandy had made many loans to friends and acquaintances who never bothered to repay him. And if that wasn't bad enough, he'd used everything they owned as collateral for his many foolish business ventures. Hoping to shield her from the problem, Eilley sent Persia to board with friends in Reno. Then she began selling off her precious furnishings and everything else in her pitiful attempt to hang on to her beloved home. Still, it wasn't enough to cover the mountain of debts Sandy had so carelessly left her.

Just when she thought she might recover from the financial disaster, Eilley received word that Persia was gravely ill in Reno. She tried desperately to get to her daughter in time, but Persia died while she was en route.

Washoe Valley was sweltering under the intense July heat, but so overcome with grief, Eilley barely noticed. Oblivious to the ribbons of sunlight that filtered through the parlor, she barely acknowledged the large group of mourners who'd come to Persia's funeral that afternoon. As her child's eulogy was delivered, Eilley sobbed softly in the back of the room. Her life would never again be the same.

The Bowers Mansion grave site. *Photo by Bill Oberding.*

The graves of Eilley and Sandy Bowers. *Photo by Bill Oberding.*

After the funeral, Persia was buried beside Sandy on the little hill overlooking the mansion. The *Gold Hill News* of July 15, 1874, reported:

> *Everyone acquainted with the kind old lady, Mrs. Bowers, will sympathize with her in her misfortunes. Since the death of her only remaining child, Persia, she has been almost crazed with grief, and some consider that it will take many months, if not years to efface from her memory the sad scenes through which it has been her lot to pass. Her husband lies buried on the hillside in the rear of the house, Persia next and her youngest next to hers. The position of the bodies suggests the rest and peace beyond the graves which it is impossible to find here. We learn that it is Mrs. Bowers' intention to lease the Mansion for a term of five years and to leave Washoe Valley for a time at least.*

Her family was resting on the hill; someday, Eilley would rest there as well. But for now, she would try to keep the mansion safe from her creditors. She muddled through her days, swearing that the spirit of Sandy stood by her side and guided her in the decisions that were suddenly thrust upon her. Unfortunately, death had not improved Sandy's business acumen. Eilley had sold all the treasures she'd held dear, and it still wasn't enough. In a fit of rage, she pulled up plants and bushes and poured boiling lye on the lush ivy she'd so carefully brought back from her European trip. If she couldn't live in her home, she'd make sure that no one else enjoyed its gardens.

When it became clear that she could no longer meet her financial obligations, Eilley was forced from her home over a $10,000 debt. Myron Lake was the mansion's new owner. As he made arrangements for the mansion, Eilley slipped into a life of ridicule.

Since her death in 1903, a glowing green apparition has been seen walking the grounds of Bowers Mansion late at night. Some believe this is Eilley. Children visiting the mansion during the day have reportedly seen Persia as well. The following story centers on the painting of Persia that hangs in Bowers Mansion. When she took her four-year-old daughter to the mansion, a woman was amazed as the little girl pointed to Persia's painting and said, "That's the girl in the living room. She told me she used to live here."

Several years ago, a friend and I sought and were granted permission to conduct a daylight investigation of Bowers Mansion. Daylight might not sound like the best time to do a ghost investigation to you, but to us it was better than the "No way" response we had expected. We assembled our small group of five and headed for the mansion. It was one of those spring days when the sky is an intense blue and snow glistens high atop Mount Rose, one of those days when it's good to be alive and in the Reno area. Would Eilley meet with us? Like everyone else, we'd heard the stories, but we wondered it the place was even haunted.

Our tour guide met us at the door and gave us a quick rundown on what we could and couldn't do during our investigation. Then she led us through the mansion, telling us about Eilley and about Sandy and Persia, as well as all the money that had passed through their hands, all the money it took to design and build this home. The library was interesting in that, according to our guide, neither Eilley nor Sandy could read. The books were meant only to impress. Other historians have disagreed, saying that Eilley was not illiterate. Either way, the library was impressive.

The psychics in the group moved to the painting of Persia. She was, we were informed, very much attached to this home. Was Sandy? Not so much. And Eilley? Oh yes, she was also attached to Bowers Mansion. We called out to Eilley and Persia and any other spirits that might like to converse with us via our old-school tape recorder, which was high tech at the time. We walked up the stairs. How many times had Eilley Bowers ascended these very stairs? The psychics immediately stiffened. Someone was here who didn't necessarily belong to the mansion but was very protective of it. No, we assured this someone, we had not come here to do any harm to this beautiful place. The tape recorders were turned on again. "Did you care to tell us your name?" Trite question, but there you go—it's not always easy to think of what to say to a ghost.

On playback, some of us thought we heard the words, "Don't you know?" And some of us thought the words were "Don't let go."

We didn't have a clue—unless it was Eilley herself. But the voice sounded masculine, and there was no Scottish brogue. Did she speak with such a brogue? Maybe it was Sandy or some other spirit just having some fun at our expense. We didn't have all day, so went back downstairs and explored the sitting room, where a crystal ball rested on a pedestal. It was so Eilley but also probably nothing like this room looked like when she lived here. Our guide said as much. We did a bit more recording and took a few more photos, and then it was time to make our way up the hill to pay our respects to the Bowers family in their final resting place.

Later, the psychics said they felt that although Eilley and Persia had been near, they had chosen to stay back and observe us rather than come forward. "The next time," someone in the group said hopefully.

Will there be a next time? Doubtful, but you never know.

EPILOGUE

As I said in the beginning of this book, ghosts and history go hand in hand, and since history is always being written, I believe we can expect more and different ghosts to appear as time goes on. Does this mean that some of those depicted in these pages might one day choose to move on? It's possible. The old saying "Nothing is ever certain but change" applies here. In the meantime, thank you, dear reader. I hope you will continue to enjoy your endeavors into your favorite location's historical past and your quest for ghosts.

INDEX

ABOUT THE AUTHOR

An independent historian, Janice Oberding is a past docent of the Nevada Historical Society and Fourth Ward School Museum in Virginia City. The author of numerous books on Nevada's history, true crime, unusual occurrences and hauntings, she speaks on these subjects throughout the state. Her "Ghosthunting 101" and "Nevada's Quirky Historical Facts" classes for Community Education at Truckee Meadows Community College have been well received.

Visit us at
www.historypress.net

···

This title is also available as an e-book